D1826025

Lost and found

Lost and found

Christ's teaching on evangelism

Kenneth H. Good

 **EVANGELICAL PRESS**

EVANGELICAL PRESS
12 Wooler Street, Darlington, Co. Durham, DL1 1RQ, England

First published in the USA by Backus Book Publishers,
Rochester, NY, under the title *Christ's teaching on the theology of
evangelism*
This edition © Evangelical Press 1990

British Library Cataloguing in Publication Data
Good, Kenneth H.
        Lost and found.
        1. Bible. N.T. Luke. Parables — Expositions
        I Title
        226.806
ISBN 0 85234 276 4

Scripture quotations in this publication are from the Authorized
(King James) Version

Printed in Great Britain by Cox and Wyman Ltd, Reading

Contents

Preface

Christians who are identified as fundamentalists, conservatives, or evangelicals have many different convictions with regard to some elements of doctrine and more aspects of service, but they are united in the conviction that evangelism is a priority in their practical application of the gospel. The implementation of the Great Commission, given by Christ at the close of each Gospel and in the first chapter of the book of Acts, stands at the head of their list of things to be accomplished for the Lord.

Irrespective of their differences in patterns of witnessing, the proper format for an 'evangelistic meeting', or the biblical method of carrying on missionary work, they all agree that evangelism is a priority which cannot be displaced by other considerations in the agenda of work to be done. For this reason various denominations with differing ideas on the subject of ecumenical evangelism will unite in popular city-wide evangelistic efforts despite the misgivings that some may have with regard to the propriety of co-operation with theological liberals.

A considerable amount of ink has been employed, and many debates have been conducted (both formally and informally) on the proper methods to use in evangelism. Calvinists have clashed with Arminians over this subject in every generation, and libraries are well stocked with treatises from both sides of the argument. It is evident that Christians who believe in evangelism do have serious reservations about some forms of it which are currently being employed.

One of the most interesting aspects of this ongoing controversy is the fact that in most of it the foundational teaching of Christ has been ignored. Paul informs us that 'If any man teach otherwise, and consent not to wholesome words, even the words of our Lord Jesus Christ, and to the doctrine which is according to godliness...' we are to 'withdraw' ourselves from such (1 Tim. 6:3-5). It is evident that the apostle regarded the teaching of Christ on all subjects as foundational to everything else. It is baffling to observe that much of the controversy about the various aspects of evangelism does not investigate the foundational teaching of our Lord on this subject.

It is an axiom clearly established and generally held that what one does is controlled by what one believes. Theology determines practice. The methods employed in various churches and missionary societies to carry out our Lord's Great Commission reveal their theological convictions. Therefore, since the methods used differ so widely and have been the subject of considerable controversy, it is bewildering that so little attention has been given to the passage in which our Lord sets forth the theology of evangelism.

There is only one place in Scripture where this is done in a complete form. While other passages in the Gospels make some reference to the matters referred to in the first part of the passage under consideration, it is only in Luke 15 that we discover a complete theology of evangelism. Here our Lord sets forth the viewpoint of each person of the Trinity in the winning of souls. Here the warmth of personal involvement is combined with the absolute certainty of the divine sovereignty. Here we learn that a commitment to the doctrines of grace is not incompatible with dedication to the work of evangelism.

We live in a time of considerable confusion in many areas, but nothing has been more perplexingly bewildering to the average person than the chaotic array of various Christian enterprises all claiming to be engaged in evangelism, but each radically differing from the rest of the crowd in important principles and methods.

Nothing will resolve this problem short of an agreement upon the theology of evangelism. Nothing is so calculated to establish this theological perspective as is this central teaching of Christ on the subject. While the entire New Testament is filled with many truths and principles which definitely bear upon the question, this fundamental teaching of our Lord is foundational to all the rest. A neglect of this passage will set us seriously off course in all our endeavours.

This exposition of Luke 15 is an attempt to relate this basic instruction to the practical work of evangelism. It is inseparably connected with other passages of Scripture, and some of these are investigated, but the primary purpose is to examine carefully the meaning of the parable in the teaching of Christ and discover how it relates to our endeavours in his service today.

Kenneth H. Good
May 1990

In appreciation

To our gracious Lord for his enabling following a severe illness which, according to the physicians, should have either taken my life or left me totally unable to function, either physically or mentally; to my devoted wife, who received so much blessing from the original presentation of these chapters as spoken messages, and consistently encouraged their publication in this form, and who painstakingly reviewed and proof-read the manuscript, making many helpful suggestions; and to my loyal friends, Ron and John, who have made it possible that this and my other writings should be published for others to read.

1.

A revelation of the heart of God

What has come to be called 'the Great Commission' appears five times in the New Testament (Matt. 28:18-20; Mark 16:15-16; Luke 24:46-49; John 20:21-22; Acts 1:8). Whatever instruction the Lord may have given about evangelism prior to his death and resurrection, the specific commandment to take the gospel to all nations did not come until after he had died and risen from the dead. There was no mandate to take the gospel to the world until the gospel of grace had actually come into being through his redemptive work; and even then it was not to start until the advent of the Holy Spirit. From then onwards redemptive faith would no longer be an *anticipation* of what God had promised; but it would be in *realization* of what he had already done in Christ.

While many people had trusted in God and had been justified by faith throughout human history from Adam onwards, they were brought into this experience by a faith that looked *forwards* to what God had promised he would do. In Christ's ministry before the cross there were many who came to believe upon him, but he constantly reminded them that 'The Son of man must die, and be risen from the dead.' All saving faith before the accomplishment of the actual work of redemption had to be anticipatory. Global evangelism, as we think of it in Christian times (including the announcement of an *accomplished* redemption), has no Old Testament precedent,

although there were certain prophecies that foreshadowed this
before the first advent of Christ. There was also a prophet
(Jonah) who had been sent to a non-covenant people typifying
the eventual inclusion of 'all families of the earth'.

But the Great Commission to go to 'all nations' and
'every creature' with the message awaited the accomplishment of the epoch-making work of redemption and the institution of the New Covenant. This, having been finished on the
cross and certified by the resurrection, must now be carried to
all mankind. Our Lord had taught his immediate followers the
principles which should govern their understanding of the
Scriptures. He had given them in parabolic form many of the
guidelines for an understanding of the gospel, when finally it
would actually be accomplished in his great work of redemption. They could now examine these tremendous facts in the
light of what he had already taught them, and, by the ministry
of the Spirit, come to an understanding of the proper
interpretation of the facts of the gospel.

Following his resurrection, and in view of his accomplishments on the cross, he gave the great evangelistic commission. Many related guidelines appear earlier in the Gospels, but the climactic and all-inclusive instruction to carry out
his work on a global basis was not delivered until just before
his ascension. This places an especially important emphasis
upon what we usually term 'the Great Commission'.

The significance of this appears in two related facts.
Firstly, it was not given to his followers until he had accomplished the redemption of his people on the cross and the
Father had certified the validity of that act in raising him from
the dead. Secondly, it was given in direct connection with the
promise of the Spirit's advent, which had been secured in the
redemptive act. The Spirit would provide the guidance and
power for this strenuous task which was obviously beyond
human capability. The Great Commission was delivered to the
disciples of Christ between the time of his resurrection and that
of the coming of the Spirit. The second person of the Trinity

was about to leave this world and return to heaven. The third person of the Godhead was about to make his advent into the place thus vacated. There was a brief period (ten days) between the two divine accomplishments in which the embryonic 'church' waited in the appointed place, governed by an attitude of prayer.

The fivefold repetition of the missionary commission must be interpreted in the light of what our Lord had taught before it was given. The work of evangelization begins with the preaching of the gospel. How that gospel is to be understood, proclaimed and expounded can be drawn from the previous training provided by our Lord during his earthly ministry. The great evangelistic parable recorded in Luke 15 is doubtless one of the passages most directly connected with this.

A careful study of the epistle to the Romans readily demonstrates that Paul conscientiously followed the doctrines and principles previously introduced by our Lord himself in such parables as the one under consideration. While Paul and other apostles expounded the gospel along these lines in their epistles, it is important to examine the parable given by our Lord himself. This provides the basic source material for some of the writings that include this teaching. Nothing written by any apostle transgresses the truths already established by our Lord's teaching while on earth. Although the New Testament writers develop certain themes beyond what Christ taught personally during his sojourn below, it is instructive to observe that usually their instruction in the epistles is actually a development of what Christ had already said.

The relationship of the parable (Luke 15) to the doctrines of grace developed at length by the apostles (especially Paul) may readily be seen by a study of this parable itself. It is significant to observe that this was what Christ taught about his salvation while on earth some fifteen centuries before John Calvin came upon the scene. The doctrines of grace did not begin with that eminent theologian, but with our Lord himself.

Christ was, and is, the great revealer of God (John 1:18). As such he is the exegete, the expositor, of the very heart of the Father. If someone seriously desires to know how God feels about man in his utterly lost condition, he must study carefully the reaction of our Saviour when confronted with the evidences of man's rebellion and unbelief. He must also studiously meditate upon Christ's actual teaching on the subject.

In Luke 15, and closely related passages (e.g. John 10), Christ fulfils the text given earlier (John 1:18) and reveals the heart of God towards the sinner. In the parable recorded by Luke we may discover the concern and activity of all persons in the Trinity for the lost sinner.

The unity of the parable

A. Its structural unity

Luke 15 records *one* parable, not three. It is to be considered
as a unit rather than as a collection of different, even though
related, accounts. The word 'parable' appears only once, and
in the singular (v. 3). While there are three distinct stories, the
transition from one to the other is carried on easily and without
a break with such words as 'Either what woman...' or 'And he
said, a certain man had two sons...' (vv. 8, 11).

The three stories all relate to the same subject. Each one
reveals the loving heart of God towards the sinner and his rejoicing over the repentance and return of that object of his affection. The shepherd invites his friends with the phrase,
'Rejoice with me.' The woman utters the same words upon
finding her coin, and the father declares, 'Bring the best robe,
and put it on him... and let us eat and be merry.'

In two instances our Lord specifically stated that there
was great joy in heaven over a sinner who repented and
returned (vv. 7, 10). While each story has a different revelation
concerning the activity of God towards the sinner, they all
have the identical sequel. God rejoices in the accomplishment
and application of his redemption in the experience of his
creatures.

Christ was telling out the very heart of God in accordance

with the general statement of John regarding his ministry as
the one who reveals God (John 1:18). He was indeed setting
forth God and making him known. This becomes a wonderful
blessing to the believer who may then rejoice in the fact that
his heavenly Father also experiences 'great joy' in the accomplishment of his plan regarding the ones whom he purposes to
save.

B. Its doctrinal unity

The doctrinal unity of the parable consists in the fact that it sets
forth the concern and the activity of the three persons of the
Trinity in the salvation of sinners. The Son is pictured first (vv.
4-7) as the shepherd; the Spirit is illustrated next as the light
(vv. 8-10); and the Father is depicted finally as the father with
two sons (vv. 12-32).

    In the story of the lost sheep (vv. 4-7) attention is directed
to the seeking shepherd. This sets forth the motivation and
goal of the Good Shepherd in giving his life for the sheep and
the Great Shepherd in caring for them. The Son is brought into
focus, and much may be gleaned from a study of this brief
section of the parable.

    In the story of the lost coin (vv. 8-10) attention is focused
upon the operation of light in locating a coin which had been
lost and finally found. Here the quiet but effective work of the
Spirit is illustrated, and similarly, much can be gained from a
careful consideration of the qualities of light as it relates to
evangelism.

    In the story of the lost son (vv. 11-32) attention becomes
fastened upon the father and his manner of receiving the lost
son who returns to the fold. As we shall see later on in the
exposition of the parable, most of the verses are concerned
with this aspect of the parable.

    Clearly our Lord desired to set forth the heart of God, as
Son, Spirit and Father, and in that order. The reasons for this

become apparent when the text is examined more closely within its context. No doubt the greatest difficulty arises with the largest and closing section of the parable. A proper understanding of the first story is greatly assisted by our Lord's words elsewhere regarding the shepherd and the sheep (e.g. John 10). It therefore presents no great problem. Likewise the second is facilitated by the references and inferences in Scripture to God as light. The exposition of this story provides no formidable difficulty.

Many evangelistic sermons have been preached from the story of the prodigal son, and doubtless the gospel has often been presented through this passage. Many exhortations to revival have been directed to backslidden believers from these verses of our Lord's parable, and doubtless many have been restored by this ministry of the Word. There have been occasions when the account has been used to teach the final restoration of Israel from 'the far country' in an eschatological sense, and there may possibly be an application to that theme of the principle involved, although only indirectly.

Problems of interpretation

If we begin with the premise that Christ is setting forth the gospel to sinners, as the context indicates, then we must assume that the primary interpretation of the third story also speaks of the Father's heart of concern for the lost son and his activity upon the repentance of that returning errant one. While that opens up many avenues of tremendously interesting features of the doctrines of grace, it still leaves a problem with respect to the repentance of the prodigal. Why does no one seek for him? How is it possible for a sinner to 'come to himself'? How could an unregenerate person have any memory of what it was like 'in my father's house'?

Granting that it is one symmetrical parable on the same subject from three different viewpoints, we are faced with the difficulty that while the shepherd sought the lost sheep and the woman sought the lost coin, no one is commissioned to seek for the lost son. Knowing what we do from the other Scriptures that the unregenerate sinner has 'no good thing' in himself and cannot create a repentant heart by his own determination, but that both repentance and faith are gifts of God, how is it possible that the prodigal could 'come to himself' and remember something of what life was like in 'my father's house'? Above and beyond that, how could he determine of his own volition, 'I will arise and go,' or 'I will say…'?

These, and other related questions, will be considered

carefully in turn when the exposition of the third part of the parable comes before us. Actually it is necessary to understand the first two sections properly in their respective settings before we can arrive at a right understanding of the problems which confront us in the third.

This is a difficulty often faced by those who would attempt to expound Luke 15. Their hearers have already had it fixed in their minds that the prodigal son represents an erring Christian. Probably the cause of the dilemma has been created by the prevailing tendency on the part of many to preach from the story of the prodigal son without taking into consideration that it is only one part of the whole parable, and that the parable deals with sinners who repent, rather than with erring saints who go astray. This is not to suggest that there are not basic principles which are applicable to the wandering Christian. Indeed, much commendable pastoral work has been accomplished by applying these same principles to the case of true Christians who fall out of fellowship with the Lord and who are subsequently brought back into that relationship by true pastoral preaching and counselling.

However, it must be remembered that this parable was deliberately spoken to, or in the presence of, people who were on the outside of this blessed fellowship (vv. 2-3). It must also be borne in mind that twice our Lord, in his own application of the parable, referred to sinners who repent (vv. 7,10).

There is a problem in the interpretation of the third section of the passage. If we understand the first and second stories to be pictures of the sinner's salvation, by what principle of interpretation can we maintain that the third is a picture of the believer's restoration? Consistency would require that the same principles be applied equally to all three portions, seeing that the entire passage is a unified whole.

Bible students have frequently discovered that those very sections of Scripture which seemed, at first reading, to present knotty problems were at the last the very sections which were rich mines of golden ore. But mining for valuable ore does not come easily. Hard spiritual and mental work is sometimes involved. Problems can become blessings if pursued properly. This will be our goal as we proceed.

Analysis of the parable

The parable may be analysed as to its contents. In doing so we may observe the following:

1. Each object was originally possessed and subsequently lost:
    a. The sheep was lost through its own act of stupidity.
    b. The coin was lost through the act of another.
    c. The son was lost through his own wilful rebellion.
    (In this we see three explanations for man's lost estate.)

2. Each divine loser is emphasized in the parable:
    a. The shepherd shows God's Son in redemption.
    b. The light shows God's Spirit in illumination.
    c. The father shows God's heart in reconciliation.
    (In this we see the threefold work of the Trinity.)

3. Each story is necessary to present the whole picture:
    a. The seeking shepherd — the devotion of the Son.
    b. The searching woman — the urgency of the Spirit.
    c. The solicitous father — the love of the Father.
    (In this we see the heart of God told out in love.)

The position of this parable in the context of Luke's Gospel is also indicative of its intended meaning and usage. Christ had just given a series of parables (Luke 14:7-33) in response to the stated unbelief and animosity of the Pharisees (vv. 1-6). The parables of the ambitious guest, the great supper, the tower and the war were concluded with the words: 'If the salt have lost its savour, wherewith shall it be seasoned? It is neither fit for the land, nor yet for the dunghill; but men cast it out. He that hath ears to hear, let him hear' (vv. 34-35). The Pharisees symbolize the hypocritical unbelievers with a visible profession and no heart for God. Our Lord pronounced a fearful warning upon all such. This immediately precedes the parable under consideration.

It is also of interest to observe what follows this extended parable of Christ. He first addresses his own disciples (Luke 16:1-13) and challenges them regarding their primary devotion, which must be vastly different from that of the Pharisees. He then turns to 'the Pharisees also, who were covetous' (v. 14) and speaks rather severely to them before giving the story of 'the rich man and Lazarus'. This is interrupted only by the very brief statement concerning those who break God's law of adultery, as though to include them in the account which follows.

The passage concerning Dives and Lazarus has sometimes been interpreted as a parable, but the passage does not anywhere include the word 'parable'. It is undoubtedly better to conclude that in this account our Lord was simply drawing aside the veil that hides the invisible world from the visible. He was putting into words what his spiritual vision embraced in the land beyond the grave. He could see what ordinary men could not, and from his vantage-point, in grace, he desired to warn them of the ultimate end of all who persist in rebelling against God's clear revelation (Luke 16:29-31).

The context of Luke's Gospel indicates that the fifteenth chapter, containing the parable of God's grace, is bracketed by notices that people who are not recipients of this grace must perish under divine judgement. The parable of the lost things is therefore a remarkable account of the doctrines of grace, as they relate to all three persons of the Godhead, and as they contrast with the fearful estate of the people who have never known God's unmerited favour.

Our Lord chose to reveal this marvellous exposition of God's grace to sinners against the background of their fearful condition. Seen in that light, this portion of Luke's Gospel becomes one of the most evangelistic portions of our Lord's parabolic teaching. It also illustrates that true gospel teaching and preaching must include the doctrines of grace if it is to be faithful to its calling.

A theological definition of the term 'gospel of Christ' must include the doctrines of grace. Apart from these revealed truths any 'gospel' that is preached publicly or taught privately must be seriously defective. A true doctrinal exposition of the 'gospel of Christ' will be inseparably welded to these revelations. Attempts to execute the Great Commission cannot be wholly biblical apart from the understanding of what the gospel actually is and how it works, both of which have been provided in our Lord's teaching, and nowhere more graphically than in this parable.

The parable of the lost things was directed to a specific group of persons. Luke 15 begins with the words: 'Then drew near unto him all the publicans and sinners for to hear him. And the Pharisees and scribes murmured, saying, This man receiveth sinners, and eateth with them.'

Immediately Luke adds, 'And he spake this parable unto them, saying...' Here the allegory begins. Obviously the parable was directed to the Pharisees who objected to grace. Our Lord deliberately speaks to them about grace abounding to the chief of sinners. In this sense, it could be said that this parable is our Saviour's defence of the doctrines of grace in the context of gospel preaching. Nowhere else in his messages were these doctrines of grace made clearer than here. Nowhere does he preach the gospel more completely.

One often hears that preaching the doctrines of grace is

contrary to evangelism. Because of this some who actually believe in these truths have a great tendency to 'hide their light under a bushel' because of a fear that preaching these things will discourage evangelistic effort, or at least confuse the sinner or stumble the weak saint.

The contemporary climate in popular Christian circles is often adverse to preaching on these doctrines. When a pastor attempts to do so he is often severely criticized by hearers who wrongly imagine that he is opposed to biblical evangelism. Their problem is that they have confused what the Bible actually teaches about 'soul-winning' with what current well-known voices are saying.

Modern religious people who oppose the preaching of the doctrines of grace make two rather serious blunders. First, they ignore the fact that it was our Lord himself who set the example of preaching the gospel in the context of these sovereign grace themes, and second, they forget that some of the greatest evangelistic preachers of the past have consistently set forth these things to the unregenerate or taught them to immature Christians. To discount the fact that Christ so preached and taught is to question the methods of our Lord himself! To ignore the history of evangelistic preaching and its results is to reveal one's ignorance of Christian history.

It is to be hoped that this present study will not only increase our zeal for witnessing and evangelism, but that it will also reinforce the faithful preaching of the doctrines of grace.

The great missionary apostle stated, 'For I am not ashamed of the gospel of Christ: for it is the power of God unto salvation to every one that believeth...' (Rom. 1:16). Granting that this gospel is 'the power of God', we must take great care that we present it in its purity. While we pray for revival in our land it would be well to examine the gospel which was preached early in the eighteenth century by the men who were leaders in 'the Great Awakening'. If we do, we shall discover that it was in conformity with this parable.

2.
Christ reveals his own heart

The characterization of Christ as a Shepherd has been a great favourite of Christians in all ages since he walked among men on earth. Countless hymns and poems have been composed upon this theme. Numerous works of art have depicted him as Shepherd, and spiritual sermons on this subject never fail to comfort believers. Some of the most poignant representations to be seen in the catacombs are rough drawings of the Shepherd and his sheep on the walls or the sarcophagi.

The favourite psalm of believers in all ages of church history has been the classic twenty-third. The New Testament contains numerous references to our Lord as Shepherd. The Gospel writers refer to Christ as one whose perception of the people of Israel was in terms of sheep without a shepherd (Matt. 9:36). He described himself as the Shepherd (John 10:2, 11, 14). The apostolic writings refer to him in this role (Heb. 13:20; 1 Peter 2:25). The New Testament contains forty-three references to the word 'sheep' and most of them refer to God's elect as the special object of the Shepherd's concern.

In the New Testament Christ is pictured as the Shepherd in three different aspects. As the Good Shepherd he gives his life for the sheep (John 10:11). This speaks of the cross. As the Great Shepherd he cares for the sheep (Heb. 13:20). This speaks of the crook. As the Chief Shepherd he will return for his sheep (1 Peter 5:4). This speaks of the crown.

There are three psalms in the Old Testament which correspond to this threefold picture of Christ as Shepherd and they come in this same sequence. Psalm 22 is the psalm of the cross. It predicts many aspects of the crucifixion and is quoted in the New Testament as being fulfilled at Calvary. Psalm 23 is the psalm of the crook. It describes the intimate relationship between shepherd and sheep, the security and fellowship made possible in this intimacy, and the assurance that the shepherd provides for his own. Psalm 24 is the psalm of the crown. It describes the entrance of the shepherd into the possession of the kingdom. These things may be more readily grasped when set out visually in the table below.

Aspects of the shepherd seen in the Psalms

Psalm	Implication	The shepherd's ministry
22	Crucifixion	Gives his life
23	Resurrection	Provides his care
24	Glorification	Establishes his kingdom

A careful examination of the four verses which comprise the story of the shepherd and the lost sheep (Luke 15:4-7) reveals many things about the doctrines of grace in our salvation. The passage may be outlined very simply. First, the sheep was lost; second, the sheep was found; and third, the sheep was restored.

The sheep was lost

As has already been pointed out, each of the lost objects in the parable sets forth a particular aspect of man's lost condition and his need for salvation. While the prodigal son possessed intelligence, he had no wisdom, and so was lost by his own wilfulness and rebellion. The coin had neither intelligence nor wisdom, and was lost wholly by the act of another. The sheep became lost by a foolish act of its own stupidity.

The lost estate of the human race is a fact clearly established in many places in the Scriptures. The New Testament attributes this lost condition to a number of things. Sometimes it is is presented as a consequence of Adam's sin (Rom. 5:12-21). This is illustrated by the lost coin, where the act of another was responsible. At other times our lost condition, or at least our aggravation of that fearful state, is traced to our own wilful rebellion (Rom. 1:18-32). This is illustrated by the lost son. And at yet other times our lostness is traced to our own stupidity in spiritual matters (1 Tim. 1:13). To gain an adequate understanding of the seriousness of our lost condition in nature it is necessary to consider carefully all three aspects of it.

A careful examination of the sheep's condition provides us with a number of graphic illustrations of the sinner's condition before his rescue by the Shepherd.

1. The sheep was entirely culpable

The sheep could not shift the blame onto someone else. While
the Lord's parable does not provide us with information on
how the sheep became lost, our common knowledge of these
animals suggests that in all probability it wandered off through
inattention to where the rest of the flock were grazing and
where the shepherd was leading. The sheep may have been so
intent upon its own nourishment that its eyes were taken off the
shepherd. In any case the blame must rest upon the sheep that
was lost and not upon the shepherd or others of the flock. It
certainly cannot rest upon the shepherd, whose greatest concern was the welfare of the lost one, as is demonstrated in the
sequel.

2. The sheep was altogether ignorant

Here we see the lost estate of those who never within themselves entertained any conscious thought of being lost. They
have not deliberately set out in life to arrive at a lost condition,
being ignorant of the fact that they were already in that state.
Actually they do not become conscious that they are lost until
much later in their experience. Probably not before some
calamity befalls them do they awaken to discover that they are
in a helpless condition and do not know the way home. This is
typical of young people who have been reared in a generally
Christian environment. Often they are totally unaware of their
lost condition, having assumed that their upbringing was guarantee enough of their spiritual safety. By comparing the par-
allel account in Matthew's Gospel in its context (Matt. 18:11-
14) with this portion of Luke's parable, we are enabled to see
this interpretation of the story of the lost sheep.

Youg people, having been reared in an atmosphere of
Bible reading, prayer and conformity to regular church
attendance, are often unaware that they are spiritually lost.

They frequently rest more upon the fact that they have never consciously rebelled against God or his commandments than on any sense of definite spiritual communion with him. In their ignorance of the danger of this condition, they move along undisturbed by conscious thoughts of judgement or eternity. Often some cultural or ritualistic ceremony has been interpreted as a fulfilment of God's will, and their salvation is assumed. When baptism has been granted to young children immediately after such a public expression of emotional commitment, and without sufficient instruction or examination, they are often given an assurance of salvation which is altogether misguided. This misconception is not confined to those churches which emphasize ceremonial conformity as the guarantee of salvation. It pervades the nonconformist churches as well.

When people grow up in the context of an assurance based upon ritual, and are later given authentication of this by education or ceremonial confirmation, without any dynamic experience of intellect, emotion, or will, they are likely to assume that they are not *really lost*. These people are depicted by the lost sheep of our Lord's parable. They possess a psychological and religiously cultural assurance of salvation, but they are actually as lost as was the sheep in Luke 15. The parable was originally given in the presence of the religious leaders who specialized in this form of theology and practice.

One of the worst features of the sheep's precarious position was that it was unaware of its danger, of who was to blame for it, and of how to be rescued from it. That awareness would eventually arrive, and it would be the first indication that a work of grace was beginning in the heart. But at the beginning of this experience, the sheep was unconcerned about such matters. Any suggestion to such a person that he was in a precarious position because he was lost would probably be met with resentment. The young person reared in a context which provided human assurance of salvation would retort that he had been baptized in infancy, or that he had 'gone forward' as a teenager. Probably he could produce some kind of record to 'guarantee' his non-lost condition, whether it be a 'baptismal' certificate or a note on the fly-leaf of his Bible with an appended date of verification.

This is not to suggest that children cannot be consciously and definitely converted as a result of an early regeneration, but it is to affirm that late twentieth-century evangelism counts far too many young children as genuine converts and additions to the church. More careful attention to the scriptural evidences of genuine spiritual life (as for instance in the First Epistle of John) should be investigated before converts are counted and baptism is granted. Some 'lost sheep' imagine that they are 'in the fold' because they have confirmation by ritual, certificate, or voice of the church organization. Many who have no heart knowledge of Christ in redemption experience are in a precarious position.

This part of the story also depicts the sad state of much of our contemporary society. Concerned only with his own immediate affairs, devoted to the search for a little more temporary satisfaction in life, and dedicated to the quest for material benefits, modern man has become so preoccupied with the natural world that he has stupidly lost his way. Any attempt to invade his little self-generated kingdom with the alarming news that all is not well and that he faces serious consequences unless he is rescued by God only generates ill-will and self-justification, unless his heart has been prepared by grace.

3. The sheep was entirely helpless

Again, our Lord does not provide us with detailed information upon the exact physical situation of the lost sheep. We may deduce from the natural world, as well as from other Scriptures, the pitiful estate of the lost one.

We are told by those who have studied the breeding, care and nurture of sheep that these animals are the most helpless creatures. They require the constant attention of shepherds. Sheep are defenceless against predators. Unlike the wild beasts who are naturally equipped with both tooth and claw, sheep will ordinarily fall victim if preyed upon, since they have no natural defences provided. Different from many of the forest creatures, they are unable to race swiftly out of danger.

The safety of sheep lies in the faithfulness of their shepherd and not in themselves. Their vulnerability is a frequent theme of the Old Testament pastoral scene.

The rescue of the sheep was entirely the work of the shepherd. No indication is given in the text that he 'heard its cry', this idea having been derived more from hymns than from Scripture. The work is uniquely that of the rescuer, with no assistance from the rescued.

A popular idea in modern religion is that our spiritual rescue by Christ is more or less of a co-operative action. The Good Shepherd is pictured as one who has done all that he can, and now the next action is up to the lost person. The sinner must give some signal to God that he is willing to be saved. He is depicted as being not altogether helpless. There is some action — however slight — that he is able to do and thus co-operate with God. Whether that action be the cry for help, the decision to believe and trust, or the manipulation of one's own emotions to the pitch of remorse for sin, the lost person feels that he must hang on to some small thing in which the action of rescue is not totally from God alone. Only divine, intervening grace can alter that deception.

The Lord's story of the lost sheep contradicts this modern theory. The sheep did absolutely nothing to contribute to its own rescue. The sheep was found and restored by actions completely outside itself. Everything that was done was accomplished by the shepherd. The sheep was completely passive in the rescue operation.

The sheep was found

Attention must be directed to the action of the Good Shepherd because he is the principal character of the story. So much emphasis has been placed upon the lost sheep in sermon, poem and song, that it has inevitably resulted in a detraction from the person of the Lord. However, Christ directed attention principally to the rescuer, rather than to the rescued. A careful examination of the few verses devoted to this account will reveal the fact that most of the words describe the thoughts or actions of the rescuer, and no information is given about those of the sheep. The inner thoughts of the recipient of salvation are depicted in the third narrative.

Three observations can be made concerning the emotions of the shepherd.

1. He was deeply conscious of the lost estate of one sheep

The 'ninety and nine' were temporarily set aside because of the shepherd's total commitment to the one 'which was lost'. This speaks of our particular redemption. It is not sufficient that we be able to know and to sing that 'Christ died for sinners.' We must come to an awareness that Christ 'loved *me* and gave himself for *me*' (Gal. 2:20).

The believer finds great comfort and assurance in the knowledge that his salvation is very personal. Not only would it have been necessary for Christ to have gone to Calvary to save each of us individually, but he actually and consciously took each of us into himself when he took our place on the cross. Such knowledge is too high for us to comprehend, but we are assured in Scripture that it is true. Just as man cannot comprehend God, neither can he understand his works. But what we cannot penetrate with our minds we can accept in our hearts, and worship. As has been so often repeated, 'What is darkness to my intellect is sunshine to my heart.'

Christ died for the elect very personally. This was no impersonal payment of a general summation of our collective guilt such as a generous benefactor or philanthropist might express towards a hapless group of people, to be appropriated by them individually at will. It was no mere payment of the corporate guilt of the elect. While it was all of that (2 Cor. 5:21), it was also far more. Some believers have lost the assurance and joy of their salvation when they became 'lost in the crowd' after they have been saved. This frequently happens when Christians become involved in doctrinal studies to the neglect of their personal devotional life in fellowship with Christ. With the welcome revival of the doctrines of grace among churches, some have become so intellectually involved in the truth of Calvinistic teaching on salvation that they have been entrapped in mere doctrinal scholarship. Preachers and teachers can become so absorbed with the intellectual comprehension of the true doctrine of salvation and its defence that they neglect our Lord's command to 'feed my sheep'. When that happens the food is placed too high for the sheep to reach it.

Lost in the wonder of the truth of particular redemption as a valid doctrinal position, they become more or less absorbed in the objective aspect of the doctrines of grace, merely intellectually conceived. They are happy to be 'of the elect' and generally rejoice in their knowledge of this and related truth. However, right here a danger may arise. The biblical truths of the doctrines of grace, intellectually conceived, provide tremendous food for deep thought and spiritual philosophy. Those whose personalities respond to scholarly pursuits and logical interests will discover great satisfaction in this contemplation. But their devotional lives may suffer as a consequence because of neglect. The brain is nourished, but the soul is starved.

In this way many have been 'lost' after they have been 'saved' — not that their salvation has been forfeited as per the notions of some, but that their spiritual lives have been crippled. They became 'lost in the crowd' of the elect. Salvation ceases to be a perpetual wonder and a subject of deep humility with high praise. Satisfaction thereafter becomes more a matter of intellectual comprehension than of vital spiritual communion.

Persons who entrap themselves in this snare will lose the sense of joyful praise and worship. No longer does the heart respond to the wonder of such expressions as are contained in 'Amazing Grace', 'Majestic sweetness sits enthroned', or 'O sacred head now wounded', as the saints sing them together. The soul does not break into joyful praise when a preacher or teacher presents Christ in a way that touches the 'inner springs' of consciousness. All becomes as silent within (and as expressionless without) as the quietness of an august library, filled with knowledge but dead as paper and ink. There is a form of intellectual legalism which is quite orthodox in doctrine but lifeless in experience. It is to be feared that this is the plight of many today who are identified as confirmed believers in the doctrines of grace, but who have become 'lost' in mere intellectualism after they have been saved. When the heart no longer sings, the mind will eventually stagnate.

2. He made the rescue of one sheep the highest priority on his list of responsibilities

Various interpretations have been attached to the fact that the shepherd left the 'ninety and nine in the wilderness', but it does not lie within our perspective to digress in pursuit of a fit interpretation or application of this phrase. In no case does the difference of understanding detract from our main purpose.

It will suffice to observe that all other ministries and responsibilities which Christ assumed and discharged were subservient to the principal end of redeeming the elect. Before his birth the psalmist had predicted that the Saviour's coming was for the purpose of redemption (Ps. 40:6-8 as understood in the light of Heb. 10:5-14). In immediate connection with his birth the angel promised that he would redeem his people from their sins (Matt. 1:21). During his earthly ministry he repeatedly referred to his impending redemptive death (John 10:1-18). After his resurrection he taught the disciples that this redemption should now be preached in all the world (Luke 24:46-49). All of this was understood as being the means by which he would glorify the Father (John 17:1-5).

The shepherd of our Lord's story is presented as one who concentrated upon a single object — that of saving one lost sheep. The gospel of redemption is individualized in this story of Christ, as it is in all the rest of the parable. There was only one sheep, one coin and one son under consideration. Redemption is applied to particular individuals.

While many believers have been limited in their understanding of this amazing truth, others have discovered the joy and comfort which are found in knowing about abounding grace in our redemption, both accomplished and applied. Where a deficiency in instruction has at some time cost them the joy of their salvation, there is great need that the souls of

these people be fed with 'bread from heaven' for their continued sustenance in spiritual life. No portions of Scripture are so
richly productive of this as are those which reveal the Lord
Jesus Christ in his concern for the lost on an individual basis.
Much benefit may be derived from those New Testament
accounts which portray our Lord's dealings with single
individuals.

It is refreshing to contemplate how he frequently met the
need of *one person* in the midst of a general clamour for his
attention. Such was the case with the nobleman whose son he
healed, the woman with the issue of blood, the Syrophœnician
woman, Zacchæus, the paralytic at the pool, the paralytic let
down through the roof, and many others. The proper biblical
reaction against the generally prevailing scepticism of modern
life has sometimes resulted in a mere intellectualism in doctrine which is sterile. This parable of Christ is a fitting antidote
to this malady. The gospel of Christ is *personal*.

3. He would not give up his search until the sheep was found

The words of the story state that he must seek '…until he find
it'. This speaks of the effectual call of God. Christ said
elsewhere, 'My sheep hear my voice and they follow me.' It
is impossible that this could fail. There is no possibility that
one of his sheep would fail to hear his voice. This brings to our
attention some weighty concepts which sometimes trouble the
minds of God's people. The effectual call of God is emphasized in this section.

1. It implies that all of the elect will be saved. The application of the gospel to the souls of men in an effectual way is
not left to chance nor to the fickle will of man. All for whom
Christ died will be brought safely into the fold. The Good
Shepherd will seek the one lost sheep 'until he find it'. It will

be returned to the fold. There is no possibility that this could fail of accomplishment, or the grotesque concept of failure on the part of Christ threatens our understanding.

2. *It implies that the gospel will go to all of the elect.* The redemptive truth must go to the ends of the earth inasmuch as there are elect in '...every kindred, and tongue, and people, and nation' (Rev. 5:9). Paul, realizing this, was willing to suffer during his ministry since he knew that he endured '...all things for the elect's sakes, that they may also obtain the salvation which is in Christ Jesus with eternal glory' (2 Tim. 2:10). This has been the true missionary motivation.

3. *It implies that the great movements of the gospel throughout the past two millennia have been sovereignly arranged by God.* He sits in complete control of the movements of nations. He providentially arranges the various interactions among countries that will enlighten one and darken another. Christ will both seek and find his sheep, and if nations need to be moved in order to accomplish that, God's purpose will be completed. The entire Roman Empire was moved in order that our Lord should be born in Bethlehem of Judea rather than in Nazareth where Mary lived. To accomplish that, 'There went out a decree from Cæsar Augustus, that all the world should be taxed' (Luke 2:1). As a consequence, thousands of families were moved regardless of the inconvenience, and thus our Lord was born in Bethlehem. The same truth applies with respect to his later searching for the sheep. A careful study of history from the first century until now will confirm this principle as valid. World history covering the last 2,000 years should be interpreted from the Christian perspective as God's control of the nations in order to bring the elect sheep into the fold. The alternative is to interpret history on a purely naturalistic basis, leaving God's sovereignty out of the picture altogether. Informed Christians will not accept this materialistic view.

4.   No national power can thwart the purpose of God in the gospel. This is true of the actions of nations, and it is also true of the responses of the human heart. Missionaries are often concerned about those nations that are currently 'closed to the gospel'. Perhaps they are not so 'closed to the gospel' as they are tightly shut against what has been traditionally considered 'missionary work' within their borders. National objections to what we call 'missionary work' are often levelled at the classic image of Victorian and Livingstonian vocation rather than against the gospel itself. In some countries, suspicion of imperialistic political aims regards the traditional missionary as subversive. But the apostle Paul, our exemplary 'missionary', would have escaped that when he invaded some terriories under the occupational designation of 'tentmaker'.

5.   No one who is upon Christ's list as a sheep can fail to arrive in his fold safely. Our Lord sought the sheep until he found it, not merely until the sheep made a decision. Modern evangelistic effort makes much of 'decisions'. The basic assumption is that man 'decides for Christ' or against him — that the entire matter lies within the will of man to determine. However, there is no word in the text that the shepherd approached the lost sheep with an option. The sheep was not asked whether or not it desired to be rescued. When the shepherd had at last found the lost one he very simply and directly 'layeth it upon his shoulders rejoicing'. The sheep had no decision to make! After all, it belonged to the shepherd by right of ownership.

Benjamin Keach, a Particular Baptist writer of the seventeenth century, understood this meaning of our Lord's words. He wrote, 'Christ finding his lost sheep, and taking it up in his arms, denotes grace, such grace that the sinner cannot resist or withstand; not that he forces the will, for that is to destroy the nature of that noble faculty; but he sweetly inclines it, overpowers it, and makes the unwilling will (that was so naturally) to be willing in the day of this his power.'[1]

Modern evangelism's nervous hyperactivity, in attempting to do that part of our Lord's work which he specifically declares is reserved to himself alone, is responsible for many serious blunders in the evangelistic ministry to individual souls. Many spiritual and psychological tragedies are strewn in the wake of some of these well-intentioned but self-appointed workers whose doctrinal understanding has been sorely neglected. Manipulation of the human emotions on a purely psychological level (albeit punctuated with an abundance of pious references to Scripture) has severely damaged the cause of biblical evangelism in contemporary society.

The sheep was restored

Salvation restores all that had been forfeited in the lost estate. There are more words employed by Christ to depict this aspect of the story than any other. Here is the primary emphasis of this part of the parable. Indeed, the restored sheep was placed in a position above the one which preceded its straying from the fold. A number of precious concepts are brought to mind in this imagery.

1. The sheep experienced a new relationship with the shepherd

While it had previously just been a part of the flock, it now rests on the shepherd's shoulders. This speaks of the relationship which flows out of experienced redemption. It must be observed that the Lord had said that the shepherd already possessed the sheep. It was his before it was lost, while it was lost and after it was found. But its latter end was infinitely greater than its former state. This speaks to us of sovereign election.

The shepherd did not find a goat and miraculously transform it into a sheep. He owned the sheep before it was lost and then he lost it. This speaks of the fact that the elect were known to God from all eternity and were registered as sheep long before their realization of it. Christ made a number of references to his possession of the sheep as his own, even before their conversion. Modern thought usually runs in the channel that we become sheep upon 'accepting Christ', even though the Scripture never uses that terminology.

In John 10, the great chapter on the Shepherd and the sheep, Christ said several things to indicate that the sheep were his before they came to know him. Speaking of the elect Gentiles who had not yet heard the gospel, he said, 'And other sheep I have, which are not of this fold...' (v. 16). Since they had not yet been converted where the gospel had not yet gone, it is evident that they did not become sheep by believing. But Christ already had them in his possession in some way. This could only have been by sovereign election.

Speaking of the Jews who would come to follow him, he later said, 'My sheep hear my voice, and I know them, and they follow me' (v. 27). Lest anyone suppose that we become sheep by hearing and following, it is necessary to observe the preceding statement: 'But ye believe not because ye are not of my sheep, as I said unto you' (v.26). The average person in today's 'gospelized' society has a different philosophy because he has been misguided by a message which says that people become sheep by hearing, believing and following. That is quite the reverse of what Christ actually said. He stated that we give evidence of already being sheep when we believe and follow.

Sometimes in Bible conference ministry I have made a test of people's understanding of this by conducting a simple experiment. While people were asked *not* to look at their Bibles, I have deliberately misread this text to say, 'But ye are not my sheep because ye believe not.' Then I would ask them, 'Did I read it correctly?' It is amazing to discover how many people believed that I had. Of course, this was immediately put right and they were then asked to look at the text while it was read again, but this time, properly. So often the faces of the whole assembly expressed consternation upon their discovery that they had always read the text wrongly in their minds and had paid little attention to what our Lord actually stated, in spite of the words he used. This is typical of believers who have been mistaught about the doctrine of election. They can read texts which contradict their views and honestly believe that the words they read say something which is quite different from what they actually see.

People who are sheep (i.e. elect) will believe in Christ when they hear his voice in the gospel (John 5:24). This cannot fail. Our Lord seeks the sheep 'until he finds it'. A proper understanding of this truth which Christ taught would eliminate many of the manipulative devices to which some modern pastors and teachers often resort in their methods of 'soulwinning'.

Before this rescue the sheep was lost. There can be no question about that. In each of the stories Christ uses the term 'lost' (Luke 15:6, 9, 24), and there is no minimizing of that truth. However, whatever was lost remained the property of the owner throughout. The sheep still belonged to the shepherd while it was lost, the coin was still the woman's while it could not be located, and the son was still the son of his father while he was in 'the far country'. The ownership of the lost object was based upon rights of possession which had been established at the time of either purchase, gift, or creation.

When the sheep was rescued it lay upon the shoulders of the shepherd. This is the position of his strength. Salvation is a mighty work of God, whether we think of the initial accomplishment of it in the cross, the continued application by the crook, or the consummation in the crown.

Lying upon the shoulders of the shepherd, the sheep need 'fear no evil'. But the sheep is also close to the ear and the voice of the shepherd. From this blessed position the sheep may have the assurance of being immediately heard, even in the slightest whisper; he is also conscious of the words of the shepherd, even though spoken in low tones. This speaks of our communion with Christ, and depicts the intimate personal relationship that is possible between our Lord and his people.

A mother will wake up in the middle of the night at the first sounds of distress from her new-born baby. This is merely on the natural plane. Our Lord hears our spoken or unspoken cry of suffering because this is on the spiritual plane. His heart is touched with the feeling of our infirmity. This is too intimate a matter to be analysed coldly by theological or psychological rationalization. The proper biblical reaction against the prevalent materialism has caused many people who love the doctrines of grace to lose their balance. Their insistence upon the truths of God's sovereignty in salvation has often led them into an intellectualism which is devoid of personal communion with Christ. So often they know the doctrines of grace but not the grace of the doctrines. This is indeed strange, since many of them rely heavily upon Puritan writings as ammunition against Pelagian errors in doctrine and practice, and the devotional depth of the Puritan writings is well known. How is it possible that such avid students of the Puritans could have missed the Puritans' warmth of love for the Saviour?

The answers may be as many and varied as there are people who hear the question, but one principle seems to run throughout them all. It is that of *legalism*. When the truth assumes a legalistic colour and people are examined upon that hue and shade rather than upon the truth itself, then the dreadful disease has begun. When we begin to examine each other on the basis of *light* rather than of *life*, and make no room for differences of expressions, terms, customs, etc., then the virus has infected the body, artificial walls are constructed, and the body of Christ is fragmented.

Although I am a confessed, committed and outspoken Calvinist, I have had the privilege of ministering in churches or congregations which were confessedly Arminian, and have often found more evidence of true spiritual life among some of them than in some churches which were quite critical of anything beyond their borders which they construed to be Arminian (by their own definition). Man is prone to create all kinds of shibboleths, and none is so keenly demanding about it as the self-appointed Calvinist who is willing to go to war with a brother at the slightest provocation because he does not 'know the doctrines', or more likely, the books and authors that are upon his 'approved' lists.

It is but a short step from hypercritical Calvinism to destructive Pharisaism. The remedy for this malady is to arrive at more emphasis upon the relationship of the rescued sheep to the Shepherd on whose shoulders he is being carried to the Father's house. Lack of this perspective in preaching and teaching is responsible for a considerable amount of ship-wreck in Christian work today, both in private lives and in public assemblies. While any particular emphasis can become Pharisaic, none is so destructive as a cold, intellectual and hypercritical Calvinism which has lost vital fellowship with the divine Shepherd. The very rightness and biblical ortho-doxy of the doctrines makes it a keener blade with which to inflict psychological wounds on their brethren in the Lord.

2.   The sheep was in no danger from enemies

Before its rescue the helpless sheep was vulnerable to attack from all kinds of predators. The lions and the bears of ancient Israel preyed upon the flocks of the people. David spoke of this with regard to his own experience (1 Sam. 17:34-36). Peter warns that the devil, as a lion, is seeking hapless sheep whom he may devour (1 Peter 5:8). The only possible reason why an individual sheep will 'fear no evil' is because of the shepherd's care and invincibility. The sheep has no strength against its natural enemies. Its safety depends upon its position with regard to the shepherd.

Following this imagery the story is told of the believer who had a keen sense of the Lord as Shepherd and who meditated much in the Psalms, especially the twenty-third. This believer often spoke of his joy in the experience of sensing reality in his 'walking with Christ'. This is not different from the testimonials one often hears regarding fellowship with Christ, and it is a scriptural experience to be desired and cultivated. However, this believer went through some extremely trying times which were continued over a long period when the magnitude of the difficulties overwhelmed his soul. Friends deserted him and erstwhile comrades turned aside. He was crushed to the point of despair. In his spiritual and emotional misery he felt that there was no hope. However, true to his pattern of thought in happier days, he turned his attention to the Psalms, especially the twenty-third, with the prayer that God would somehow restore his soul.

In this condition he returned to the meditation about 'walking with Christ' which had been so much of a comfort in past days. Once more he thought of his walking with the Lord, and in a reverie or half-dream of imagination, he envisioned the two sets of footprints in the sand which had been a familiar mental concept in days gone by.

But suddenly intruding into the picture was the spectre of his present mental anguish over the experiences of the recent past. He had been deeply hurt by others in an extremely unfair way. So much did this intrusion disturb his mind that his mental imagery responded and the picture changed. Instead of two sets of footprints there was only one in his 'dream'. His immediate emotional reaction to this self-induced imagery was one of petulant complaint. 'See,' he said to himself, or to the Lord, 'I had to walk alone through all of this trouble.'

However, in the realization that he was being more influenced by his own imagination than by the actual language of Scripture, he turned to the New Testament to find Christ's own words about the shepherd and the sheep. Coming to our passage, he noted that the shepherd, having found the sheep, did not merely walk side-by-side with the rescued one, but that he 'layeth it upon his shoulders'. There was obviously a position even more blessed than walking by the side of the Lord.

His meditation continued in the revised imagery according

to Christ's own words. It seemed to the despondent believer that the Lord was telling him that 'Yes, there was indeed only one set of footprints at a certain place, but *they were not yours. They were mine.* That was when you were so weary, tired, bruised and ill of soul that I carried you.'

The believer was so overwhelmed with the realization of Christ's love for him that he dissolved in tears. Now the phrase of his favourite psalm came with renewed force: 'He restoreth my soul.' The darkness was dispelled.

3. The sheep was brought safely home

There was no possibility that the sheep would fail to arrive safely at the haven. That was assured on the basis of Christ's work, not that of the sheep. In his position of security, comfort and communion, the rescued one may be certain of his sure arrival in the Father's house.

While there is great comfort and blessing accruing to the believer in this biblical account and the doctrine which it illustrates, it is to be feared that many believers do not enter into the realization of the joy of which our Lord speaks. It must be observed that Christ here spoke of God's joy, not ours.

The story tells us that the shepherd rejoiced at the finding of the lost sheep (v. 5). We are also told that upon his arrival home he called in his friends to say, 'Rejoice with me' (v. 6). Then in Christ's application of the story, he pointed out 'that likewise joy shall be in heaven over one sinner that repenteth' (v. 7). Three times the word for rejoicing is used, and each instance suggests the emotion of one of the persons of the Godhead.

The joy of the shepherd at finding the lost sheep indicates the tender affection of the Son for his sheep. The joy of the friends and neighbours suggests the response of the Holy Spirit through his people at the return of the lost one to the fold. The 'joy in heaven' pictures the restrained way of speaking of the Father which is typical of Scripture. But more of this in the second section of the parable.

We may be assured that God rejoices in the salvation of the lost. The parable may actually be considered as Christ's revelation of the heart of God with respect to this relationship. Each section of it contains considerable notice of this fact. In each instance neighbours and friends or members of the household are called in to celebrate the return of the errant one, and the entire scene is one of great delight over this fact.

True believers are especially responsive to this aspect of evangelism. At the human level, no more poignant memory of spiritual awakening is possible than the recollection of those who came to Christ during times of true revival. The emotional response of believers to the evangelism of the lost is clearly pointed out in this parable.

However, this is at once both the strength and the weakness of the church. During times of spiritual refreshing when the saints are truly revived and sinners are being saved, the church becomes 'mighty as an army with banners'. Rejoicing is evident on every hand and is reflected in the hymnody of such times.

But this very strength can become a vulnerability. Many church members live in past memories. They can remember when there was much genuine rejoicing over the conversion of sinners, baptisms and additions to the church. A genuine spiritual nostalgia occupies much of their consciousness. They long for a return to these truly 'good old days', and frequently, the over-usage of the term 'old' in connection with this disposition is found to punctuate their speech patterns. It is not always intelligently spiritual. There is a large content of sentiment which often overcomes the normal processes of thought to the detriment of a proper, biblical conclusion.

This concern with the blessings of the past may be entirely beneficial. God sometimes awakens his people through the memory of good things which have now passed away. Israel was called upon to remember better days and contrast them with current backslidings. The church may likewise be challenged to review the past and consider how far she may have fallen from those standards. All of this is positive and scripturally legitimate. It is employed by our Lord in his letter to the seven churches of Asia (Rev. 2;3).

However, it is to be feared that many have succumbed to some very substantial dangers and are presently in jeopardy of exchanging shallow emotion for genuine spiritual responses of joy. In some instances this has already happened, and in others it is a threat of disaster for the future. The church which lives only upon a repetition of emotional 'highs' resembles the teenager who greedily devours huge quantities of 'empty calories' without properly nourishing his body. A future illness can safely be predicted.

The desire for a return to the 'old' days when spiritual awakenings brought much joy and power to the church is entirely understandable, but in all too many instances Christians have not used proper discernment in evaluating current movements which purport to produce this. In some cases churches and their pastors have been greatly misled into adopting measures which seemed to produce the external evidences of these 'revivals'. If a time of genuine revival has been experienced and later periods of spiritual lethargy and backsliding come, the great temptation is to resort to mere psychology in an attempt to restore what is remembered. Frequently Christian workers are unable to distinguish between what is merely a resuscitation of nostalgic memorabilia and what is unpretentiously spiritual. Both Satan and the flesh are great imitators of the genuine work of God. When they are combined, a masterpiece of deception may be produced.

Spiritual joy is a fact of Scripture. This is evident in both Testaments. Our Lord's parable under consideration lays emphasis upon the rejoicing which properly takes in the conversion of sinners. Nothing is more spiritually and psychologically uplifting to a congregation of believers than to see

God glorified in the salvation of sinners and then to see these new converts baptized and added to the church.

But these things can be imitated and Christians can be deceived into thinking that their churches possess the genuine evidences of spiritual progress when such is not the case. It must be remembered that Christ also spoke of the seed which fell upon stony ground and 'sprang up' without delay. However, having 'no root', it quickly died (Mark 4:5-6). His explanation of this parable tells us that such people receive the word 'with gladness'. Luke's record describes these 'believers' as people who 'receive the word with joy ... for a while believe, and in time of temptation fall away' (8:13).

There is a 'faith' which is not genuine. Some call it 'historical', indicating merely an awareness of the biblical facts of history or doctrine. Some refer to this as mere intellectual assent, much as one accepts the general facts of national or global history. There is no personal trust involved.

It is quite possible with modern methods of mass communication and psychological manipulation to gather large crowds of people together to 'hear the gospel', when that 'gospel' carefully deletes most or all of the doctrines of grace. It is also possible to form large organizations which promote this form of activity in which the emphasis lies upon man rather than upon God. We must remember that the parable under study focuses attention primarily upon the one who rescues the sheep.

During the years of the great controversy in the denominations between the modernists and the fundamentalists there was little, if any, emphasis placed upon the distinction between genuine revival and its counterfeits. However, the issue of that struggle, as it continued for some decades, left many Christians without the experience of genuine church revival in the traditional sense. They had come through years of controversy and combat with no significant organizational victory. The large denominations and their institutions had been lost to liberalism or to highly organized religious hierarchies. They had seen very little of significant gospel victory. They were longing for some visible evidence that this gospel for which they had so earnestly contended was indeed capable of achieving victory in the areas of their defeat.

The weakness of the churches lay in the very area of their concern for the lost and their emotional attachment to remembered revivals or accounts of genuine spiritual awakenings of the past. Thinking in terms of the crowds that attended the preaching of Spurgeon or the genuine awakenings in the ministries of Edwards or Whitefield, they looked for such in their own times, praying earnestly that it might happen. I remember having been in prayer meetings where there was considerable agonizing over this matter, and hearing the earnest pleadings, 'Lord, do it again! Do it again!' into which I entered most heartily, and would do so once more, should the occasion arise.

This earnest desire was genuine and is not to be taken lightly, neither should it be discarded in discouragement. There is definite reason that the churches should continue to pray for revival which would follow the principles of the doctrines of grace as revealed in this parable. However, to settle for an imitation or a substitute is virtually the equivalent of asking for bread and receiving a stone, or requesting a fish and accepting a serpent (Matt. 7:9-10). It can be assumed that neither stone nor serpent comes from God.

Churches and Christians in the latter part of the present century are being bombarded with the latest techniques of merchandising things called 'missions' and 'evangelism'. Intimidating figures are paraded with these methods under the general aura of success. Impressive programmes are advertised with the latest approaches to the general public. Legions of Christians and many churches are being swept along with this tide. The impression is conveyed that this is the 'revival' for which we have prayed. The 'joy and rejoicing' are evidences that our labour has not been in vain. God is happy and so should we be. Fundamentalism's lean days are over; evangelicalism's poverty has turned to prosperity. The tide has at last turned in our favour, But are these things true? Many are acclaiming them as real. Others are not so sure. Still others are certain it is all delusion.

Upon sober reflection and a more careful analysis of these trends along with our Lord's words in this parable, an increasing number are loath to give assent, or even to join in the singing. They are suspicious that the 'revival' may be in reality only a stone and not a piece of bread — that it did not come from God — that it is a poor imitation of reality. It may even be a serpent which will fatally strike its host after all.

Christ reveals his own heart

Application

Following the exposition of this part of the parable it is necessary to devote attention to the abiding lessons, or the problems to which the truths may be applied. There are two aspects of the present account which have especially pertinent meaning for our times.

1. Christians and churches should enter into the concern of Christ's own heart for the lost sheep

The apostle Paul experienced this. Speaking of his driving motivation in his ministry, he said, 'The love of Christ constraineth us...' (2 Cor. 5:14). Referring to his own suffering in this ministry, he wrote, 'I suffer trouble, as an evil doer, even unto bonds... Therefore I endure all things for the elect's sakes, that they may also obtain the salvation which is in Christ Jesus with eternal glory' (2 Tim. 2:9-10). Referring to his experience in fellowship with this heart concern of our Lord, he said of himself, 'Who now rejoice in my sufferings for you, and fill up that which is behind of the afflictions of Christ in my flesh for his body's sake, which is the church' (Col. 1:24).

The apostle's consciousness was so dominated by his

consuming passion to identify with Christ (Gal. 2:20) that he actually experienced some of the same emotions which moved the soul of our Lord when he contemplated the lost sheep. This is not to suggest that Paul's sufferings in any sense contributed to redemption, as the Roman Catholic teaching of supererogation maintains, but that he had so entered into the heart of Christ's passion for the elect that he experienced similar emotions in his soul. Paul's agony was but a small drop in a limitless ocean, and in no sense redemptive. However, the question needs to be asked, 'Do we understand anything of this in our own experience?'

This concern for the lost sheep, involving possible consequent suffering, should permeate the minds of believers and churches. It is experienced in various ways. A believer may be called to a mission-field which involves both mental and physical suffering, but in the process he may locate some of the 'lost sheep' who will hear and believe. In his thoughts about his life of privation on some remote mission-field he rejoices because God's purpose for his life has been fulfilled, and trusts that in it all God has been glorified. A believer may be stricken with some disease or accident which requires his hospitalization in pain and suffering. However in this stay in hospital he may become friends with one or more of the lost sheep and lead them to a knowledge of the Lord. In retrospect, he views the experience as arranged by God. Or again, perhaps under governments dominated by anti-Christian powers, a believer may undergo much mental and physical persecution. But through this experience he may be thrown into prison along with some of the 'lost sheep' and have the privilege of bringing them the knowledge of the Good Shepherd. His attitude towards his persecution and suffering will follow the pattern already established by Christ. He has entered into the 'sufferings of Christ' towards the finding of the lost sheep, the elect.

2.   Christians and churches should be aware of the imitations of this concern which have pervaded modern Christendom

So much has already been said about this danger in the exposition of the parable that it is unnecessary to repeat the material here. However, one point needs to be made in conclusion. Since all actions seem to have a corresponding reaction, it is also possible for sincere believers to become cynical in attitude towards all popular, well-advertised and successful movements of missions and evangelism. The attitude is sometimes generated that anything which is successful with regard to numbers or finances must be erroneous in character. Many who love the doctrines of grace have a tendency to draw general conclusions that if a church or a ministry is apparently successful it must be partially heretical. We must avoid this negative partiality which is based upon our limited experience.

It is undoubtedly true that the gospel in a true context of the doctrines of grace seldom has a widespread hearing on the popular media-amplified programmes. One is much more likely to hear the Arminian emphasis either in philosophy or method. However, those who love the doctrines of grace need to be careful not to become too negative in attitude to the point of paranoia. A positive attitude (Phil. 4:5-9) is much more befitting for a Calvinist. There are at least two reasons for this.

First, God is also in control of these things. He will see to it that what truth is expressed will eventually be to his glory who makes even the *wrath* of men to praise him. He may also turn the tide in the future and men will be ready to listen to the true gospel again as once they did in the days of Jonathan Edwards and Whitefield, or Spurgeon.

Second, the West hears more truth, in spite of these distortions, than can be heard in lands dominated by anti-Christian governmental or religious forces. People in Communist-controlled nations are unable to hear even the watered-down version of the gospel presented by popular 'spectaculars'. Those whose cultures are dominated by Rome are no better off. In spite of the shallowness of the modern religious (so-called 'gospel') scene, we in the West are still more privileged than much of the rest of the world.

3.
Christ reveals the heart of the Holy Spirit

The heart of God is revealed in this threefold parable of lost things. Here Christ is fulfilling the word spoken about him by John when he said, 'The only begotten Son, which is in the bosom of the Father, he hath declared him' (John 1:18). Numerous other passages, especially in John's Gospel, declare this and related truths about our Lord as the great revealer of God.

The revelation of the Trinity in this threefold parable, and the concern of each person in the Godhead for the lost, have been noted by expositors in various periods of church history. The parable has provided material for many evangelistic messages to set forth the burden of the gospel in the context of the doctrines of grace. Not only does this passage of Scripture furnish ample content for evangelistic preaching of the highest order, it does so within the setting of the doctrines of grace. Indeed, some of the verses are the strongest illustration of these truths found anywhere in Scripture.

Man in his natural estate has many false ideas about God. Whether one studies the modern philosophers in their vague imaginations about the nature of God, listens to the contemporary pronouncements of self-appointed prophets who confidently state what God thinks and does without so much as a shred of biblical support, or consults his own emotional desires about the will of God without studying the Scripture on the subject, one clear principle emerges. Man is by nature an idolater. He creates God in his own image. But this is not the God of the Bible.

When we study the various forms of grosser idolatry found in history we are usually struck by the common factors of *ugliness*. There are exceptions to this in some of the Greek and Roman religions where natural beauty is deified, but generally the idols of the ancients were objects of considerable ugliness. Although the physical form does not necessarily have repulsive features, the moral character usually does. This is merely a reflection of man's darkened imagination.

The Old Testament is replete with God's pronouncements against idolatry. Israel was not permitted to make representations of God in any manner lest they become a snare to them. The New Testament is equally forceful in condemning idolatry, but the horizons are considerably extended into the realm of the imagination and man's erroneous concepts of deity. Every thought is to be brought into obedience (2 Cor. 10:5). We are not to trust our imaginations or our thought projections into a concept of God. Christ has revealed the Father, and we come to know God and to worship him on that basis.

In this threefold parable of Christ, the heart of God as Son, Spirit and Father is revealed in his concern for the lost. If we are to think God's thoughts after him, then we ought to cultivate a similar interest and burden. We should engage in corresponding activity. We should share the shepherd's concern, the woman's burden and the father's anguish.

Modern thought conceives of God as a weak-charactered, grandfatherly sort of benign personality, who is referred to carelessly as 'the man upstairs' or characterized in other, equally irreverent ways. In the stories which constitute this trilogy Christ reveals the loving heart of God, but there is no sense of the weakness and vacillation which are conjured up by the modern humanistic imagery. Here God's love is seen in the context of its true dignity. It is not weak, as imagined by modern thought. It is infinitely strong, and it is completely consistent with his wrath which is also revealed in other Scriptures.

In Christ's story of the woman and the lost coin (Luke 15:8-10) we have a brief parable which pictures the concern of the Holy Spirit for the lost and the way in which he activates his people to the execution of his will in the matter. The heart of God is revealed in that he energizes the church to action as a priority of the first importance. All else on the woman's agenda is suspended in the interests of locating the lost coin.

Again, the parable is best studied under the form of a simple outline. The coin was lost, the coin was found and the coin was restored. At each step we discover one of the important aspects of the Spirit's work in God's concern for the lost. However, before beginning an examination of the individual verses, we need to reflect upon the imagery and get the symbolism properly in focus.

Assuming that the parable is a threefold revelation of the heart of God, and also assuming that each person of the Godhead is revealed as to his heart concern, it is evident that this second account must speak of the Holy Spirit. There can be no question about either the first or the third story. The first and last are clearly established in many other Scriptures. But what of the second?

1. By the simple process of elimination, *there is a strong suggestion that the Holy Spirit is intended in this portion.* Trench said, 'We shall have in the three parables the three persons of the Holy Trinity, albeit not in their order, since other respects prevailed to give the parables a different succession.'[1]

2. *The Spirit is often presented in an impersonal way.* While he is definitely and unquestionably a person, equally so with the Father and the Son, yet his invisibility and the manner of his working are such that it seems to be impersonal. So much

is this the common misunderstanding that many professing Christians often thoughtlessly refer to him with the impersonal pronoun 'it'.[2]

3.   *The Spirit is frequently symbolized by light.* John's first epistle tells us that 'God is light', and this portion of Scripture, with its emphasis on fellowship, concentrates upon the work of the Spirit in the life of a believer. The woman's lighting of the candle suggests to us the entrance of the Spirit into a situation where his illumination is greatly needed.

4.   *The qualities of light symbolize to us the characteristics of the Spirit's ministry in the earth.* It would be well if the church had paid more attention to this aspect of evangelistic work during the present age. Many blunders can be avoided by giving heed to this portion of our Lord's parable.

5.   *The activity of the woman suggests to us the energetic de-votion to the task of seeking the lost that the Spirit generates in believers in times of special illumination which always accompany genuine revival.* The lethargy which has come upon the church in many periods of its long history has usually emerged because she has been 'walking in darkness'. Light brought into the scene has invariably produced a different perspective in the church's concepts and activities.

These general principles will be developed as the texts are now examined more closely.

Christ reveals the
heart of the Holy
Spirit

The coin was lost

Once again the lost condition of the sinner comes prominently
into the picture at the beginning. Several salient points need to
be observed in connection with this lost estate of the coin,
which from the context obviously represents a lost sinner who
will be found and restored. This lost condition of the coin well
illustrates man in his natural estate under the following
considerations.

1. Man is lost through the act of another

In the case of the sheep a natural tendency to go astray of its
own volition is brought into focus. In the case of the son an
attitude of stubborn rebellion may be blamed. But the coin had
neither tendency nor will. Its lost condition was not its own
choice. It had nothing to do with the matter. Action outside
itself was the sole cause of its position.

 This aspect of our lost estate in nature is set forth in
numerous Scriptures, in none more formally nor theologically
than Romans 5:12-21. Here we see that by our natural condition we are under the severe judgement of God. This legal aspect of our original condition is traced to the action of one man,
the federal head of the human race, Adam. In this we had no
decision to make. It was already established before we had
consciousness.

The universal condemnation of the race in Adam is so clearly revealed here that it is impossible to mistake Paul's meaning. A catalogue of the specific words may be important to emphasize this truth. All the descendants of Adam are judicially under the just condemnation of God, as revealed in the following words:

> 'By one man sin entered into the world, and death by sin; and so death passed upon all men, for that all have sinned' (v. 12).
> 'Death reigned from Adam to Moses, even over them that had not sinned after the similitude of Adam's transgression...' (v. 14).
> 'Through the offence of one many be dead...' (v. 15).
> 'The judgement was by one to condemnation...' (v. 16).
> 'By one man's offence death reigned by one...' (v. 17).
> 'By the offence of one judgement came upon all men to condemnation...' (v. 18).
> 'By one man's disobedience many were made sinners...' (v. 19).

It is obviously impossible to escape the meaning here. The sin of Adam plunged the entire human family into a condition of condemnation. Paul's generalization is that 'Sin hath reigned unto death...' (v. 21). The action of one person brought disaster upon all.

The lost coin represents the sinner as existing in this condition as the result of the act of another. While some may make objection that this principle is 'unfair', it should be remembered that we recognize and operate upon this principle regularly in normal society. Human experience does not contradict this law.

The illustration may be made of the young married man

who decided to change his residence to another country. Taking his wife with him, he changed citizenship and the couple settled down in the new land. Their unborn children would suffer the consequences of any errors of judgement that the parents may have made in emigrating. If we assume the subsequent birth of several sons and daughters, and if we also assume the possibility that the couple's adopted country eventually declared war upon their native land, we then see how the children (through no choice of their own) were born into a condition of enmity against the nation which was once their parents' native land. These young children, through no choice of their own, would be the legal enemies of their natural grandparents. That this scenario is no stretch of the imagination will be seen by all who have studied the history of World War II.

We enter this life on the wrong side of God's law. When the infant emerges from the womb he is forensically at enmity with God (Rom. 5:10). Elsewhere Paul speaks of our being 'by nature the children of wrath' (Eph. 2:3). While this is only one aspect of our lost condition, it is a most important one which is frequently minimized by those who have adopted a humanistic philosophy.

2. Man's lost estate becomes worse as long as he remains unfound

From the parable some deductions may be made.

First, a long-lost coin will corrode by the natural action of its surroundings. Some metals deteriorate more rapidly than others, and some environments have a more deleterious effect upon substances than others. Even so, some people naturally have personalities which are much more susceptible to their social environment than others. In addition, some societies and cultures are much more detrimental to the mental and spiritual well-being of children than others. However, a universal principle applies to all cases. The continued existence in a lost condition never improves the status of the material. The progress is invariably downward.

The children reared in an environment of strong moral convictions will not fall into open sin as readily as the ones who lack this benefit, but they are vulnerable in spite of this excellent background. Again, young people reared in the context of a society which operates on principles of moral rectitude may be preserved from open sin for a longer period than some of their contemporaries who do not have this advantage, but they are also vulnerable. There are standards, either within the individual or the society where he dwells, which retard the inevitable deterioration of the person. But apart from the miracle of being restored to its designed position in the divine plan, an ultimate disaster of soul is a final certainty.

The longer a coin remains lost, the worse its condition becomes. The gold and silver will tarnish, the bronze will corrode and the iron will rust. But beyond that, the natural accumulation of dust, dirt and debris will hide the coin from those who desire to locate it.

Anyone who has performed the odious task of 'spring-cleaning' is aware of the fact that objects long lost finally come to light as they are rescued from various accumulations of dust, soil and defilement. These objectionable substances well represent the gradual accretion of the 'things of the world' which have a strong tendency to fasten upon the one who leaves the environment of protection represented in home, family and church.

The gradual accumulation of the unwanted substances combined to make it more difficult to locate the coin. The longer a lost sinner is in the world, absorbing all the principles that surround him, the more difficult it becomes to locate him. There is nothing in the appearance of a lost sinner which indicates that he is one of God's elect. He may well be as defiled as the others among whom he lives. Thus it was in Corinth that God foretold Paul that he had many elect in that place (Acts 18:10), and the church that was eventually organized there included some believers who had been badly tarnished 'coins' in their former lives (1 Cor. 6:9-11).

3. The sinner is unable to contribute to his own salvation

The coin did not cry out to the woman who sought it. It did not have the capability to do so. Neither did it move towards the light which eventually revealed its whereabouts. This well represents the lost sinner who can do nothing on his own behalf. The light came to where the coin was 'hiding'. The light was sufficient to identify the coin in spite of whatever corrosion may have attached to its surface. It was the light in the hand of the woman that accomplished the work. The coin did nothing.

4. The sinner retains the image of God in spite of his lost condition

As a coin retains the 'image and superscription' of the government or sovereign, so the lost sinner retains something of the Creator. Moses, in recording the covenant God made with the entire human race (Gen. 9), makes reference to the capital crime of murder and locates its heinous nature in the fact that 'In the image of God made he man' (v. 6). This was stated after the Fall. Paul makes a similar statement when addressing the intelligentsia of Athens, saying that since men are 'the offspring of God' they should not imagine that idols of 'gold, or silver, or stone, graven by art and man's device' (Acts 17:29) could possibly represent the Godhead. He similarly identifies man in addressing the Corinthian church with regard to the proper order of the sexes (1 Cor. 11:7). Man, in his lost condition, still bears the image of God in some sense. In spite of the fact that the image is seriously marred by the Fall and the corruption of nature, man still possesses intellect, emotion and will. While all parts of man's nature have been seriously affected by the results of the Fall, man continues to retain these basic faculties. Adam's transgression did not eliminate the human faculties, but it seriously contaminated them.

Man is still able to gather information, classify what he discovers, and in his reasoning powers, arrive at fundamental or complex principles called 'the laws of nature'. He is able to further rationalize these principles into a philosophy. His mental powers may accomplish remarkable things in the realm of making use of this mass of data towards the achievement of desired goals. Under the blessing of God in common grace this results in benefit to society in general. However, man is not able to philosophize his way into a knowledge of God; neither is he able to master his intelligence to the point of changes in behaviour which are pleasing to God. The depravity which became universal as a consequence of the Fall has rendered him totally unable to exercise his intelligence into a knowledge of God (Rom. 1:19-23; 3:9-12).

In spite of the fact that man still bears an image of the Creator in his being, and as such continues to possess an emotional nature, he is unable to force these emotions to love God. This part of man's nature is able to produce much that is beautiful and wonderful in the realm of the arts, and, again, under the blessing of common grace, much of this is beneficial to society in general. A mother's love for her children, the beneficent attitude of philanthropists, and the common sense of loyalty or patriotism which binds a society together are evidences of this retention of the 'image of God' in human kind. Yet so definitely has the Fall contaminated the entire human bloodstream, and so much has man come under the baneful influence of his arch-enemy Satan that he is not capable of compelling his emotions to love God, even though he may know full well that this is God's requirement as revealed in both Testaments. Man is helpless to move towards God in the realm of his emotions.

There are vestigial remains of the image of God in the volitional nature of man. He can will to do certain things, or he can will not to do them. There is a vast area of life subject to this portion of man's being. So much of one's life is occupied with this faculty that man conceives himself to be virtually autonomous in all things. Since he can decide what he will wear, what he will eat, whom he will marry, where he shall live, and so on, he vainly imagines that he has the same kind of choice in things which pertain to God. But as in the previously viewed realms, there is a specific limit to man's capability which was established in the fall of the human race in Adam. He cannot will to come to God, just as he cannot decide that he will love God. He cannot 'by searching find out God'. While he is capable of many things, he is totally unable to move towards his Creator. All of his religion is nothing more than a vain attempt to escape from God, despite its high-sounding phraseology and use of chosen biblical texts.

Man is as powerless to co-operate in his own salvation as was the coin that was lost. He cannot alert the searcher as to his whereabouts. He cannot even indicate his decision as to whether or not he desires to be rescued. As the coin was completely inert and passive during the rescue operation, so the sinner remains inactive throughout the first part of the entire work of searching and finding. Here the work must be exclusively carried on by another. The coin cannot call out for help, neither can it climb back into the place where it once was. It must be located and rescued by an intelligent and concerned power completely outside itself.

This does not imply that man does not become consciously involved in his conversion. It must be remembered that the work of God in the salvation of a sinner is a complex matter involving many and varied operations. That is why our Lord devoted three different stories in this parable to this topic to bring out the full meaning of the truth. Each account in the parable emphasizes a particular aspect of the whole, and it requires all of the three to come to a full understanding of what

Christ taught here. The conscious involvement of the sinner in the conversion process does not appear until the third story is told. The first two accounts are exclusively devoted to the work of God, with man seen as altogether passive. This emphasizes the necessity of the prior work of God before it is possible for man to become consciously aware of any participation whatever. To put it more theologically, regeneration must precede conversion. While regeneration itself is not a conscious process (any more than is human birth), conversion definitely involves all three aspects of human nature: intellect, emotions and will. Confusion on this important distinction has caused many to go astray both in doctrine and in methods of evangelism or missions.

It is right at this point that particular care must be exercised to avoid the danger of human rationalization. Since man does retain the image of God in at least three principles (intellect, emotion and will), the strong tendency is to conclude wrongly that man can exercise these faculties in a Godward direction and that he can (under the proper intellectual or emotional inducements) decide for Christ.

But this does not follow the teaching of our Lord in the first two stories. The sheep makes no effort to guide the shepherd to his unhappy location. There is no outcry, no signal, no indication that he is now, at last, willing to be rescued. Neither does the coin call out to the searching woman or move out from under the debris which had hidden it. The searching and finding are exclusively carried on by another. The pitiable objects of concern are quite passive throughout the whole exercise.

Christ reveals the
heart of the Holy
Spirit

The coin was found

The identity of the woman in the parable has been variously
interpreted by expositors in the history of the church. Whatever meaning is placed upon this person must harmonize with
the other sections of the parable, as well as with the ultimate
purpose of the whole.

Remembering our initial approach to the parable in the
light of the truth of John 1:18, and knowing that the first and
third stories obviously refer to the Son and the Father (in that
order), we conclude that something in this second story must
then refer to the Holy Spirit. It is hardly fitting that the woman
should be interpreted as the Spirit, in spite of the fact that she
searches very diligently, which parallels the work of the
shepherd in the previous account.

We may be reminded that the church is presented in the
New Testament under the figure of a woman (Eph. 5:21-33),
and that in the various statements of both John and Christ, this
figure of speech had considerable foundation in the body of
teaching which the believers inherited as their legacy. Inasmuch as the church is to be filled with the Spirit (Eph. 5:18),
and in view of the fact that God is characterized as light (1 John
1:5), it is more reasonable to assume that the Spirit is not
symbolized by the woman herself, but by the *light which she
carried* and the driving urgency which motivated her actions.

This accords with the symbolism of the tabernacle, where

the lamps within the house of worship, manifesting the energy supplied by the oil, gave light to the priests to carry on their routine ministries inside the enclosure, but outside the sacred veil. As the light in the holy place illuminated the shewbread upon the table and the altar of prayer, so the Holy Spirit directs the believer-priest into his proper ministry respecting Christ and intercession. The light which the woman carried speaks of the ministry of the Holy Spirit through the fulfilment of the Great Commission in the preaching of the gospel.

Many commentators either disregard the application of the story to specifics or they ignore the interpretation of the woman and her lighted candle. But A. B. Bruce discerns this meaning and so applies it, while lamenting that the others do not. He writes, 'The finding would appeal specially to feminine sympathies, if the lost drachma was not a part of a hoard to meet some debt, but belonged to a string of coins worn as an ornament round the head, then as now, by married women in the East... This view favoured by Farrar, is ignored by most commentators.'[3]

This jewellery fashioned from coins had a far more precious significance to the woman than the combined value of the individual 'pieces of silver', which were of relatively little monetary worth. It represented to the Eastern women of that time what the wedding ring signifies to modern wives of the Western world. It symbolized her relationship to her husband.

It is not reasonable to assume that the woman's determined urgency to find the coin was based upon its mere financial value. Her zealous animation had another cause. The word our Lord uses here is unique to the entire New Testament. 'Drachma' is found nowhere else, although some six times one may locate the term 'pieces of silver'. All other places employ a word which is specifically tied to the metal used. This word is drawn, not from the Roman coinage, but from the Grecian.

Two things are suggested to our minds by the symbolism

and the unique usage of this Greek word. First, since the woman may well represent the church in this present gospel age, and the ministry of the Holy Spirit through her, the Gentile world is in view. Long before this the term 'Greek' was established as synonymous with 'Gentile'. Our Lord is looking towards the extension of the gospel into the Gentile nations and the calling of the elect from among them. Second, the value of the coin lay not in its intrinisic value, but in its importance to the bridegroom who had given it to his wife. Its monetary value was, expressed in modern terms, about the equivalent of twenty pence. A housewife would hardly initiate an urgent house-cleaning schedule of this magnitude for the sake of a lost twenty-pence coin.

Writing of this W. S. Hottel observes, 'The "ten pieces of silver" probably refer to the ten coins worn as a frontlet by the women of the East. This frontlet was given by the bridegroom to the bride at the time of marriage, and like the ring in Western life, it was invested with a kind of sanctity sacred to her. Should one of its pieces be lost, it would be regarded as an indication that the possessor had been unfaithful to her marriage vow.'[4]

In some Eastern cultures any loss from this headband of coins would signify either that the woman regarded the marriage as of little concern, or that she had been unfaithful. She would be most anxious to appear with a full count of coins upon her husband's return from a far journey. It would signify to him that she had been a faithful and dutiful wife in his absence.

Some expositors speak of the candle and the light as the Word of God, and there is much truth in this, but that misses the full symmetry of the parable where all the persons of the Trinity are seen as concerned with the rescue of the lost. It is better to see the woman as representing the church, and the light as picturing the Holy Spirit. The woman's concern to find the coin speaks of the Spirit-wrought concern within the church to engage in this important activity. The voice of the

Spirit is not heard audibly in this age, but he speaks through the ministry of the church.

A number of salient points may be made following this line of interpretation.

1. The first evidence of the Spirit's work is to awaken the church to its need

This was the work of the Holy Spirit, as outlined by our Lord in his promise concerning his Pentecostal advent. In John 16:12-14, Christ looked forward to the Spirit's coming at Pentecost and the age that would ensue. Having come, the Spirit would show Christ's followers things that the disciples were not able to understand or obey before the Pentecostal baptism (v.12). The guidance given the church during the apostolic period and recorded in the book of Acts provides graphic evidence of how he continued to direct the work of Christ after our Lord had taken his place at the Father's side in glory.

During this same period of time, and much more to the present point, the Spirit also moved the apostles to write the epistles which were directed to the church to awaken her to her need for conformity to Christ's will and purpose. Most especially, the epistles of Christ to the seven churches of Asia show forth this principle. An examination of these letters of our Lord reveals that of the seven, only two were exempt from severe rebuke and the command to repent. Seven times in the letters to the Asian churches was Christ heard to say, 'He that hath an ear let him hear what the Spirit saith unto the churches.'

The work of the Spirit to the church is to awaken her to her need and to remind her of her loss. General movements of the Spirit among Christians over the past two millennia have been generally identified as times of revival. These seasons of spiritual refreshment, such as the Great Awakening in eighteenth-century Britain and America, resulted in much effective evangelism. Many lost coins were located and restored.

2.   The next result of the Spirit's work is to awaken the church to its responsibility

When the church becomes spiritually aware that she has lost what had been her responsibility to keep, she becomes aware that this loss is a reflection upon her heavenly Bridegroom. She does not want to be 'ashamed before him at his coming', and so she sets about correcting her error and preparing for that event.

The first visible thing she does is to light a candle. If the light speaks of the Holy Spirit, this suggests that she now becomes conscious of the need for his presence, power and guidance. However, from our knowledge of how he works, we are aware from other Scriptures that even this beginning of awareness on her part was his work which he did invisibly. But now she commences a programme of searching. Her convictions are turned to organized and concerted effort. Conviction alone will not correct the condition that prevailed. She must consciously do something about her previous failure.

This speaks of activity which flows out of spiritual conviction. Churches must have more than a mere intellectual grasp of the doctrines of grace and the fact that sinners are lost. They must also come to realize that in the mass of unregenerate mankind lie some who rightfully belong to the church in the plan of God. They cannot be visibly hers so long as they lie in that lost condition, but they are judicially hers by God's elective decree. Just as our Lord spoke of the sheep which *he had* but were not of the fold of Israel (i.e. they were Gentiles who had not even heard the gospel as yet), so the church may speak of the elect who have not yet been located and brought into the circle of the church's fellowship. This was Paul's outlook (2 Tim. 2:10).

**3.   The next result of the Spirit's ministry was to enable
the church to carry on this work in spite of great
inconvenience**

Only a very few people really enjoy house-cleaning activities,
but faithful home-makers know that periodically this unpleas-
ant task must be undertaken. There are a number of inevitable
side-effects that cannot be avoided in this necessary work.

Firstly, a substantial amount of dust is raised. The Lord
said that the woman, after she had lighted the candle, swept the
house 'diligently', nor did she abate her efforts until she had
found the lost coin. The rearrangement of furniture and
continued sweeping of the accumulation of dust and dirt
caused considerable discomfort to herself and to other residents
of the home. This speaks of discipline, which when enforced
either in a church or in a home usually raises considerable dust
to the disturbance of the residents there. But it is periodically
necessary.

Secondly, other responsibilities were temporarily suspended in the interests of the overriding obligation. She *must*
find that coin which represented so much to her and her
husband. No time could be wasted now in non-productive
projects. While cooking, sewing, entertaining and similar
exercises were legitimate activities, she could not afford to
channel time and effort into lawful endeavours while neglect-
ing her predominant and urgent task.

Many churches have succumbed to the temptation to
invert their list of priorities by permitting secondary and
permissible activities to usurp the place which belongs to the
search for the lost coins among us. Pastors have frequently
been regimented into acting as managers of programmes
which in turn are supposed to manage other programmes
which they hope will keep the flock entertained and occupied
with secondary matters. Some of these highly-organized
'programme conscious' churches need to get back to the

basics and engage in a programme of 'house-cleaning' as a priority. Some of these assemblies may boast a successful programme-oriented ministry and be able to exult in numeric accomplishments, but few souls actually come to Christ in a genuine experience of conversion where a continuous diet of entertainment has displaced the spiritual preaching of the gospel.

Thirdly, pieces of furniture had to be moved from places where they had stood a long time in order to get at the dust and debris which had accumulated underneath them. This speaks of organizational reformation. Churches are much like civil governments. Agencies once created continue interminably unless drastic action is taken to eliminate what is unnecessary. Perhaps, as is often the case in house-cleaning times, a total change of furniture is beneficial. So long as organizational re-organization does not transgress the simple biblical outline of how churches should be constructed regarding membership and office-bearers, there are many variations and possibilities which could well be much better suited to the time or the place in which a church exists.

4. The Spirit's ministry enabled the church to carry on the work until the lost was found

Many programmes of evangelism have failed simply because what was begun did not continue. This is often true of various types of visitation programmes. The Lord said that the woman continued to sweep and search until she located the lost coin (v. 8). Searching for lost articles by conducting such an operation as the woman carried out requires the expenditure of considerable energy. She was tired at the end of that day, and rightly so. Searching for the lost is exacting work. Many become greatly wearied in the effort and a large percentage give up the continued labour.

Paul reminds the believers that there is a need to be

diligent in our labours. In due season we shall reap, 'if we faint not'. How often an excellent programme has been instituted in an attempt to fulfil our Lord's words in the Great Commission, but that effort has failed because the people became 'weary in well doing'!

5.   The Spirit directed this search within the house

Various interpretations have been placed upon the meaning of the term 'house'. It is the ordinary word for the dwelling, and designates what was actually the woman's sphere of responsibility. She had no authority outside this domain, but within this limited sphere she was to search and rearrange until she located the lost coin. Bearing this in mind, it may be suggested that the 'house' could represent the visible organization of a church in contrast with the world which lies outside. If that be the case, then the interpretation depends upon our understanding of what is included here. In view of the fact that this parable was spoken in a context which preceded the establishment of the church as an entity separate from the nation of Israel, the concept of the 'sphere of profession' may be indicated. The abiding principle would be that the woman was responsible to search throughout the sphere under her immediate jurisdiction, rather than elsewhere.

This suggests the aspect of evangelism which has to do with the families connected to our churches through the membership of close relatives. Every church has faithful and active families some of whose individual members may be unsaved. There are wives whose husbands have not been converted, and vice versa. There are parents who have children who have not yet come to Christ in saving faith. Paul deals with this concept in 1 Corinthians 7. Some of these persons attend the services of the church out of social courtesy and listen to the exposition of the Word of God. They are in a secondary sense 'in the house', without actually being members of the local church. Many of these persons are 'lost coins'. A church should give priority to finding these. Experience has indicated that many of these 'lost coins' are numbered among the elect.

6. The Spirit directed to the location of a coin which legally belonged to the woman

The coin was hers before it was lost, while it was lost and after it was found. She did not hasten to the money-changers and secure another coin to make it hers, substituting it in the headband which signified her faithful relationship to her husband. No other coin would do. She must find and restore what was actually hers by legal recognition.

This speaks to us of the fact that the identity of the elect lies entirely within the will of God. The actual coins which adorned the woman's person were not selected by herself, but by her bridegroom who had chosen them for her. She was responsible only to exhibit them after they had been bestowed. She could not make coins of another metal or create such an ornament of her own design. She could only wear what had been designed and bestowed on her by another. But she was responsible to keep safe what she had been given.

God plants churches through the efforts of people we sometimes call 'missionaries', although the Scriptures do not use that term. The Bible word for these church planters is 'evangelists'. These gifted men proclaim the gospel in areas to which God sends them. The elect hear and respond by coming to Christ in faith. He then gathers them into a group and organizes a church where they may worship and serve God according to the Scriptures. The evangelists' work could be summarized by saying that they 'run a gospel test' on the hearers to locate the elect. Having found them, they train them

in the truth and organize them into a church. The woman no
doubt brought the light into various corners of the house to
discover if the coin was there.

This is the first step in the fulfilling of the Great Commission. A second step logically follows. Within the circle of
the church's influence there are (or will be) others who come
into 'the house' by some physical connection to one who is
already within the fellowship (usually by natural relationship). They are in an identifiable position within God's providence, as Paul indicates in 1 Corinthians 7. The sanctification
of a spouse or a child here does not refer to that person's
spiritual acceptance into the kingdom of God by regeneration,
but to his or her special place in God's providence. He is lost,
but 'in the house', and as such under special influences which
are not extended to people out in the world. 'Unsaved loved
ones' are always high on a spiritual church's priority of prayer.
Much fruit has been borne by her attention to this important
group. We are reminded of this peculiar 'in-law' or secondary
relationship by Paul's words to the Philippian jailor (Acts
16:31) as well as his explanations to the Corinthian church (1
Cor. 7:14). While this does not indicate any covenant union
with God, it does speak of a providential relationship which
has often led to the experience of redemption.

Christ reveals the
heart of the Holy
Spirit

The coin was restored

No sooner had the woman found the coin than she requested her neighbours to join with her in the joy she experienced. Our Lord lays considerable emphasis upon this aspect of the story. Not only does the woman rejoice, she wants her neighbours and friends to do the same, and above that, 'There is joy in the presence of the angels of God over one sinner that repenteth' (v. 10).

There can be no question about the divine joy. It is expressed in each of the three stories which make up the parable. In the extended account, everyone is happy except the 'elder son', who refuses to enter into the experience in any way. Christians in fellowship with the Lord are most delighted when they see evidences of souls turning to God in repentance and faith. Nothing is so encouraging to believers who have participated by prayer or by witnessing as to see the people for whom they have made intercession come to Christ in genuine faith.

It is to be observed that the lost coin, once restored, takes up the proper function for which it was originally designed. It is now on an equal footing with the other nine. When the elect have been found they are then to assume that function for which God originally created them. Now they adorn the brow of the woman and declare to the world that she belongs to her bridegroom. A church that is lax in her responsibilities towards the 'lost coins' in her household is making an exceptionally poor representation to the world of her heavenly Bridegroom and of herself as well.

Paul pursues this theme in his great chapter on our salvation by grace (Eph. 2). Beginning with our estate in nature (vv. 1-3) and demonstrating that the totality of our being was touched with evil, the apostle goes on to speak of our estate in grace (vv. 4-9), showing that this was wholly God's accomplishment with no contribution from us. 'By grace are ye saved through faith; and that not of yourselves: it is the gift of God' (v. 8).

However, he does not proceed to another subject before pointing out: 'For we are his workmanship, created in Christ Jesus unto good works, which God hath before ordained that we should walk in them' (v. 10). God's election is not merely so that we shall be rescued from darkness and disaster. His election includes these 'good works'. It must be observed that these, as well as our redemption, are a definite part of the whole plan. They were 'before ordained'.

This is similar to the great statement of the first chapter on election where Paul says that we have been 'chosen in him before the foundation of the world that we should be holy, and without blame before him in love' (v.4). Election is not merely to salvation from destruction. Election is to a life of holiness and service unto God. The apostle also reminds his readers in Rome of this truth. After having set forth the culmination of salvation by grace through more than eight chapters of the epistle, he reminds his readers that now, in view of these recorded 'mercies of God', every believer has the responsibility to discover his place in active service (Rom. 12:1-2). We are to 'prove what is that good, and acceptable, and perfect, will of God'.

No emphasis is placed upon the position or activity of the sheep after it has been found, except that it is obviously in close fellowship with the shepherd. After its restoration no word is given about its extended position in the flock to which it is restored. But the coin is restored to its rightful place, and now is able to serve in the exalted purpose for which it had been selected. Other coins would be repeatedly exchanged in the market place. This coin would henceforth adorn the brow of a privileged woman. It may be assumed that the restored son, once back in the father's house, assumed a position of honour and service which the father had had in mind to give him; but more of this later.

Christ reveals the
heart of the Holy
Spirit

Conclusion

The woman is the only person mentioned who confesses personal culpability in the loss. While the Lord referred to the shepherd as having lost one of the sheep, this is not a confession of personal guilt. It is rather the expression of a sense of personal loss. He never says, 'which I have lost'. His words rather are these, 'which was lost'. In the case of the father, his expression includes the word 'lost', but again, he confesses no personal responsibility. He says simply, 'He was lost.'

However, in the case of the woman, she confesses before her neighbours that the coin had been found '...*which I had lost*'. She freely admits her guilt in the matter.

True revival has always affected the church in this way. There is much confession of personal guilt for failure. There is the sense of obligation to make this admission in a public way. The woman gathers people together in order to share her joy, but also so that she may make her confession before others.

The second story of the parable sets forth the third person of the Godhead in a manner consistent with his ministry during this present gospel age. While the shepherd had to appear visibly where the sheep had become lost, the father does not journey into the 'far country'. But the light must enter the scene, not to be seen himself, but to illuminate the darkness. The Spirit is unseen but is present in the world with a specific purpose — illuminating lost 'coins' that the woman will pick up and restore as a further extension of this same work of salvation.

4.
Christ reveals the heart of the Father

In order to understand the parable of the lost things it is necessary to keep in mind that it is a *unit* (i.e. one parable rather than three) and that each story is to be interpreted in the light of its position in the whole. Nowhere is this principle more transgressed than in most popular expositions of the third narrative given by Christ.

While there are abiding principles here which may be applied to many other aspects of spiritual truth in evangelistic endeavour, the primary interpretation of the third story, that of the prodigal son, must always remain true to the purpose of our Lord in the whole context. This parable was given to reveal the heart of God towards lost sinners and the activity of each person in the Trinity to accomplish the salvation of the ones whom God has chosen in grace.

Frequently, and perhaps most often, the story of the prodigal son is applied to the backslidden believer who has for a time forsaken the peace and security of the 'Father's house' for the transient joys of the world. While there are principles here which may be applied in this way, that is not the primary purpose of this account. Were this the case, it would be out of harmony with the other two portions of the whole parable. It must, according to biblical exegesis, be applied to the regeneration and conversion of a lost sinner, just as the others. The doctrines of grace lose nothing from a true understanding of this portion of Christ's teaching.

It is to be noticed that in each of the three accounts the Lord places some stress upon the condition of the object in view. The sheep was *lost* (v.6). The coin was *lost* (v.8). The son was *lost* (v.24). In addition to that, the Father says of the son that he was *dead* (v.24). This cannot possibly refer to a straying believer, but only to an unregenerate sinner 'dead in trespasses and sins'. There is more reason to apply the third section to a lost sinner than the first two, but obviously all pertain to the same object.

Consistency demands that we interpret the story of the prodigal son as the account of a lost sinner coming to Christ, in harmony with the stories of the sheep and the coin. However, the son is pictured as *active* in the conversion experience while the other two are entirely *passive*. This is not a real contradiction, but rather the same spiritual transaction seen from a different vantage-point. The narratives of the sheep and the coin represent Christ and the Spirit as active in the salvation of the sinner, who is viewed as entirely passive. The son portrays the response of the awakened sinner and his conscious activity at this point. These are only the two sides of the same picture. The salvation of a sinner is a complex action, and it requires more than one story to give the whole perspective. Christ does this by showing the activity of each person of the Godhead.

However, this brings another problem into focus. How can it be said that the lost son (if he is to be interpreted as unregenerate) 'came to himself'? (v.17). How can it be explained that he spoke of his father's house, seemingly from memory, and that he arrived at the determination to 'arise and go…'? (v.18). Does not this suggest a believer who has gone astray rather than an unregenerate sinner who has not yet come to know the Lord?

Much popular evangelical thought has made use of this story to bolster its unscriptural notions about two aspects of salvation: the idea that a person who has been in the 'Father's house' can wilfully desert those blessed precincts and return to the world and his original lost condition; or the idea that repentance and the determination to come to the 'Father's house' originate within the sinner when he begins to think clearly (comes to himself). That both of these fancies are contrary to Scripture (both here and elsewhere) will be seen as we progress with the exposition.

However, it must be noted that the preacher or teacher who attempts an interpretation which does not transgress other doctrines of Scripture must cope with the difficulties which come forward in this third part of the parable. It will be seen that the doctrines of grace are not at all contradicted by a proper understanding of this section, but that rather they are abundantly supported. However, the Calvinist must be prepared to face the misunderstandings and repercussions that will occur when Arminians respond to his truly biblical presentation. This will set forth predestination in its strongest form, which usually angers the naturalistic mind. This is of particular concern to pastors and Bible teachers who must give some thought to human reactions.

We will examine the third story in a pattern similar to the former accounts. However, since the Lord added a sequel to this anecdote, we need to do the same. The story of the prodigal son will be investigated in the following outline: he was lost, he was found and restored, he was maligned.

**Christ reveals the
heart of the
Father**

The prodigal son was lost

In verses 11-16 the Lord employed a familiar experience to describe the condition of the human race in general terms. While the sheep had been lost due to its own stupidity, and the coin had been lost because of the act of another, the son was lost by his own wilful rebellion against the government of his father's house. All three aspects of human 'lostness' are accurate and biblical. But the third story speaks most pertinently to conscious human experience.

Paul describes the descent of the human race in its wilful rejection of God's revelation (Rom. 1:18-32). All of the pieces of Christ's allegory fit into this pattern. The application is to the race as well as to the individual. Mankind is like the 'younger son' who demanded what he imagined was his by right and, upon receiving it, used it without delay to get as far away from the government of his 'father's house' as he could.

From the standpoint of creation the human race may corporately and generically be considered as God's children. This was Paul's thrust in the message to the Athenians at Mars Hill. He rebuked his idolatrous audience for their deliberate distortion of the proper concept of God, and reminded them that 'We are the offspring of God' (Acts 17:29). Idolatry was therefore a primary transgression of his law. James reminds us that mankind is 'made after the similitude of God' (3:9). There is a creative sense in which all persons are children of God, but this does not imply (or even infer) that as such they possess any of the eternal divine nature, a 'spark of divinity', or deserve anything else but God's wrath for sin. Though creatively all people are in one sense 'children of God' who bear his image or similitude, nevertheless all lie under condemnation for sin. None, in the true spiritual sense of the words, or with respect to salvation, can be considered as 'children of God'.

There are a number of ways in which men and women may properly be referred to as children of God, short of justification and regeneration. Adam bore this designation after his creation (Luke 3:38). This implies no more than that his genesis was the result of God's immediate handiwork as recorded in the early chapters of the first book of Scripture. Adam's descendants, though far from God spiritually and under his wrath judicially, still bear that image, however much it has been marred by sin. It was on this basis that capital punishment was instituted in Noah's time (Gen. 9:6). Paul makes such a generic reference in 1 Corinthians 11:7.

While it may be true that all men are the offspring of God and may therefore be considered 'sons' in the sense of mere creation, it is not to this that our Lord refers. The sonship in view is the same as that with which the parable closes. No legal change came about as the consequence of the prodigal's return. He was recognized for what he had been and had never ceased to be. The celebration at his reappearance did not make him something he had never been, nor did it elevate him to a newly received position he had never held before. He had been a son before he departed, he was a son in the foreign country, and he was still a son after he entered the father's house.

Our Lord is presenting an aspect of the gospel of which very little is heard in our times. He is pointing to the fact that the sonship of the elect is not a fact which originates in our repentance and faith, but one which had prior existence in the counsels of the Trinity. In the records of God, we are accounted as his sons before we experience the joys of this blessing. The truth of this appears in the Scriptures which refer to our election (e.g. Rom. 8:28-30; Eph. 4:4-10; etc.), and it also surfaces in the divinely controlled utterance of the high priest in connection with our Lord's sacrificial death: 'And one of them, named Caiaphas, being the high priest that same year, said unto them, Ye know nothing at all, nor consider that it is expedient for us, that one man should die for the people, and that the whole nation perish not. And this spake he not of himself; but being high priest that year, he prophesied that Jesus should die for that nation; and not for that nation only, but that also he should gather together in one the children of God that were scattered abroad' (John 11:49-52).

Evidently, in view of the man's office, which was still in force, and because of the epoch-making event about to occur, God overruled the priest's mind. While he consciously spoke what he imagined to be his considered wisdom and judgement, he quite unconsciously uttered a prophecy concerning Christ's death. John points out that this higher wisdom did not proceed from his own mind, but that it fell from his lips in view of the office he held at the time. In a few days the veil of the temple would be torn in two and the divine hand would demonstrate that the office of the earthly high priest was finished. But as a last, dying pronouncement from an office which was about to be terminated, God sovereignly controlled the utterance of truth in an *ex cathedra* pronouncement from heaven through his appointed officer on earth.

It is to be noted that the elect are here called 'children of God', when as yet they have not heard the gospel of their salvation. This was because they were so described in God's records. This harmonizes with our Lord's references to the sheep (John 10), where he speaks of the elect Gentiles as sheep that he already possessed (v. 16), even though they had not yet been born. It also harmonizes with God's word to Paul while he was in Corinth (Acts 18). There the apostle was told to continue with his ministry of gospel preaching because 'I have much people in this city' (v. 10), even though they had not yet heard the message.

It is evident that long before we heard the gospel — even before we were born into this world — we were children of God in the divine reckoning. Our names had already been entered into the Lamb's book of life at the time the world came into existence from the hand of the Creator. Certainly, if our names were entered, they were enrolled under the classification of what we would eventually become in experience — sons. While we were in sin and rebellion against God, that record was in view in glory. During the time of our wicked pursuit of the pleasures of sin, before our regeneration and conversion, the record in heaven listed us as 'sons of God'. We were not so in experience, living under the judgement of divine holiness against sin. While still in 'nature's night' we were not acknowledged as the sons of God on earth, but we were so in the divine counsels. This elective sonship must eventually be manifested, first on earth, and then in glory. We had been recorded as sons, but upon our natural birth here below we were in the 'far country'. We would be acknowledged as sons upon our coming to God in repentance and faith.

The prodigal did not seem to be a son of his father in the 'far country'. His behaviour before the 'mighty famine' denied any relationship with his ancestry. His appearance after the calamity had touched his life was equally deceiving. No citizen of the foreign land to which he had fled would have guessed his true pedigree by observing his behaviour or appearance. His whole life was a denial of his true ancestry. No acquaintance could have imagined his destiny had he observed him at the occupation of feeding swine. All we read about the prodigal during those days strongly belied his connection with 'the father's house' both before and immediately after the 'mighty famine arose'.

However, he was a genuine son throughout all those dark days. It was so, because of his father, not because of anything in himself. The record of that sonship was in the heart of his father within his true home, even though there was no consciousness of it in his own mind. For a time the son would have eradicated that if he could, but he was unable to do so. It was a fact that had been established by action entirely outside himself. His sonship was not his own doing. He did all that he could to obliterate the relationship, but he could not succeed. Had the 'far country' been destroyed before his exodus from it, he would have perished with it. But the fact is that he 'came to himself' before that happened, because of the realization of his precarious position there. Sinners who come to God are first made to tremble at the certainty and justice of their judgement. The prodigal came to to realize that he was perishing in the place where he was.

Before we enter into an exposition of this third section of the parable it would be well to observe the proportionate space devoted to the account. While the story of the sheep occupied only four verses, and the record about the coin three, that of the son requires no less than fourteen (deleting the added verses about the 'elder son'). However, since that sequel was a part of the whole, it should be included, making a total of twenty-two, which is more than five times as much as was given to the sheep and more than seven times as much as was given to the coin. For some reason the Lord devoted considerably more space to this third story than to the other two combined. There are two reasons for this.

1. This was essentially the unfolding of the heart of God as to his infallible purpose in saving lost sinners. Here we have a parabolic presentation of the same truths expounded by Paul in such passages as Romans 8 and Ephesians 1. It is a picture of the heart of God as revealed in the unfolding of his purpose as the Father of all the elect persons. It could be said that this parable was the seed of the idea for the tree of doctrinal content in the Pauline passages already referred to, as well as other portions of the epistles which deal with the doctrines of grace. It contains the strongest possible picture of the absolute sovereignty of God in the salvation of the elect. For that reason the Lord devoted more space to this part of the parable than to all others combined. The human mind does not readily receive this truth, and Christ accordingly lays more emphasis upon it.

2. This was also the revelation of the heart of the sinner in his exercise of awakened conscience in coming to the end of himself and entering into the experience of repentance and forgiveness. While the stories of both the sheep and the coin are essentially *external* with regard to the sinner, this is intensely *internal*. It is the testimony of personal salvation as it might be told in a meeting of the saints anywhere. It shows what the repentant, forgiven and restored sinner would remember of his deep exercise of soul. This fits well into the context, recalling that this extended parable was given to an audience composed of 'publicans and sinners' who had come to hear the Lord in the presence of the 'Pharisees and scribes' who were present to criticize.

The lost estate of the younger son must be examined under several considerations: firstly, the seeming contradiction of his being referred to as a son while in this estranged position; secondly, the extremity of his condition while away from the father's house; and thirdly, the severity of his conviction when he finally 'came to himself'. Each of these steps is instructive in the doctrines of grace.

The seeming contradiction

We have noted above the rudimentary aspects of this presumed 'contradiction'. It is to be observed further that in the eternal records of God, having to do with his immutable purposes, long before we ever became conscious of our election to salvation, it was so established in his heart and mind. To put it another way, æons before our advent into this world as part of the human race, it had been authorized in the divine council chambers of eternity that we would eventually come to the experience of being 'sons of God'. This is the importance of such passages as Ephesians 1:3-14, and the many other scriptures which refer to God's unconditional election of the ones he gave to Christ and for whom the Redeemer became the 'surety'.

These elect persons were called 'children of God' before they were such in experience. God was their Father, but only in prospect. However, what God purposes to do is as certain as though it were already history. Whatever is scheduled in his plan is experience in prospect. If that were not the case, Bible prophecy would be meaningless. In one sense there is neither history nor prophecy with God. All is an ever-present *now*. He lives above time, although he works in it to accomplish his will. As he inhabits eternity, he created time to be the dwelling-place of man. This is quite incomprehensible to us, but it is biblically factual.

In later New Testament passages the apostle Paul expounds upon this mystery of how God's purpose to make us his sons is brought to pass in time (Rom. 8:29-30). This design was established in 'past' eternity, but brought to fruition in time and 'future' eternity.

The primary truth expressed is that of our actual sonship in the eternal purposes of God. What had been established before we were created is now begun by the Holy Spirit and will be carried out to perfection in the future. From that perspective God may be considered the Father of all the ones he has marked out (elected) in eternity before time. In terms of their experience, they would become his sons by the Spirit's application of an already accomplished redemption. Before that actually happened and was applied they were not 'sons of God' in any visual sense. But they were 'sons of God' in the prophetic vision. There is no problem in the fact that the prodigal son was referred to as a 'son' before he 'came to himself'.

However, this does not imply that the unregenerate person, as typified by the prodigal in the 'far country', may be put into the category of a 'son' in our reckoning of Christian fellowship.

The unsaved are in the place of judgement and under the wrath of God. The Ephesians were told that before their coming to Christ they were 'children of wrath, even as others'. This teaching is completely different from the heresy promulgated by the liberals that all mankind are to be considered 'children of God' under his universal fatherhood. Indeed, this doctrine is the direct opposite of that error. It is also quite distinct from the theory of the Reformed churches which designates their 'covenant children' as proper members of Christ's kingdom while still infants, and members of the church while still unregenerate.

The seriousness of his condition

The story begins with the younger son's demand for what he considered to be his proper 'rights'. No doubt frustrated with the restrictions of the father's house, he insisted upon 'his share' before his father's demise. Apparently this had some foundation in legality or the social customs of the day, for the father not only conceded the point, but provided the means for the younger son to leave home and fulfil his own selfish desires. Though the prompt departure must have been a deep grief to the father's heart, he permitted it to happen. This took place 'not many days after', as though the son could not wait to put as much distance between himself and his father as possible. He 'took his journey into a far country'.

This is not only a graphic picture of the entire human race, it is a description of each of us individually in our attempts to escape from God's requirements of us. Man has retained much of what was originally given to him before the Fall, but he is not usually thankful for these blessings. He regards them as his 'inalienable rights'. Man has used his intelligence to create theories which widen the gap between himself and God. Much of 'higher education' demonstrates the tendency that is common to the race. Many of the creation gifts granted to man before

the Fall are still retained, though contaminated with sin. Man
ordinarily makes use of these gifts to separate himself from
God as far as possible. Rather than employing these bounties
as his Maker designed them, he uses them either to get as far
from God as he can, or to enjoy life without God in the 'far
country'. Paul vividly describes the descent of the human race
in Romans 1:18-32.

Man continues to possess many things that were granted
to him in the original creation. He can investigate, understand
and make use of much of the natural creation. However, when
he attempts to explain his own origins, it becomes apparent
that despite his great knowledge and excellent reasoning faculties he is unable to grasp the evident fact that he has a Creator
to whom he is responsible. It is amazing to discover that many
well-educated people who have an otherwise excellent capability to reason from the obvious and draw proper conclusions
are fully committed to the proposition that the origin of the
human race was nothing more than some 'fortuitous con-
course of atoms', or some inexplicable 'cosmic accident'.

The divinely given intellect of man, along with his education, is often put into the service of designing theories which
eliminate God from his own creation and consider his revelation of himself in both nature and Scripture as meaningless.
Just so the prodigal used the very possessions he received from
his father to remove himself from the paternal influence.

Man has retained an emotional nature, but usually all its
energies are directed towards self-centred pursuits. He is concerned primarily with what accommodates him, giving no
thought to what may please or displease God. Love of self is
the primary motivation, however disguised in altruistic terminology. He cannot really love God and, in the event that he is
religiously inclined, he finds it an unbearable burden to
attempt to do so, in spite of the fact that this 'is the first and
greatest commandment'. This becomes an insuperable barrier
to his tranquillity.

Man has a will which operates in self-determination. He

can make a multitude of decisions and determine which course to follow in countless dilemmas. He imagines, on this basis, that he is free to choose of his own free will to obey God. He deeply resents the message that he does not have this capability, since 'They that are in the flesh cannot please God' (Rom. 8:8).

Man is frustrated by this knowledge, and in his rebellion against what God has decreed because of sin, he invents various forms of religious theory which tend to eradicate this stubborn fact. Much religious thought (even some serious theology) emphasizes that man possesses a 'free will' with respect to God and righteousness.

While some will admit that man has no freedom to obey the *law* of God because of his natural depravity, many of these will make an exception in the case of the *gospel*. Somehow their system of thought covers all areas of human responsibility except one. According to this theory man's natural depravity makes him incapable of obeying the *law of God*, but not incapable of obeying the *gospel*. They agree that man cannot please God in *most* things, but they cannot accept the idea that this incapacity extends to *all* things. But the passage (along with corollary texts) makes no such exception.

Much evangelicalism revolves around the theory that man can 'decide for Christ' at any time he wills to do so. He can 'accept Christ' on his own schedule. But man does not become a believer in the same way in which he decides to wear a particular article of clothing or go to a certain restaurant for a meal. Modern religious thought has blundered badly in its over-simplification of this basic principle of evangelism.

This arises from a lack of understanding regarding the doctrine of human depravity as presented in the Scriptures. It confuses two things which need to be distinguished. Technically it is true and scriptural that there is only one condition of salvation — faith in Christ (e.g. John 3:16). But spiritually it is also quite impossible for man to generate saving faith on his own. Repentance (the obverse side of the coin) is also demanded (Acts 17:30). But man finds himself unable to repent or to generate faith. What is required of man is outside his ability to generate or promote. While there is no legal barrier to man's repentance and faith, there is a natural obstacle which he cannot overcome. Human depravity necessarily involves inability. The Lord Jesus stated it briefly: 'No man can come to me, except the Father which hath sent me draw him' (John 6:44).

In the case of the prodigal son, the door to his father's house was certainly open to him all the time he was absent from it. The father's behaviour upon his actual return demonstrates that. In one sense he was free to go home at any time. However, in another and more realistic sense he actually was not free to do so until something first happened within him. He was bound in his own wicked will to the point where he could not return at any time. Just so, man's depravity enslaves him, and he is actually not free at all. He is 'fast bound in sin and nature's night'. Something must happen to him before he can say, 'I will arise and go.' Short of that event, it is impossible for him to take the road home. The road was not closed; the will was unable to motivate action.

From the standpoint of moral principles the prodigal was not hindered from going home by any external force. But practically he was not free at all, since he was tightly bound by his own determination. In this condition, and lacking some influence from without, there was no possibility that he would or could make the right choice. Much of the popular emphasis on 'decisions' fails to take this into consideration. No amount of human persuasion can overcome this inborn inability to act. No training can provide the determination to move towards God. That must come from above.

While it is true that 'Whosoever will may come', it is also true that none will do so unless he is externally enabled. Our Lord not only stated, 'No man can come to me, except the Father which hath sent me draw him...' but also, 'No man can come unto me except it were given unto him of my Father'

(John 6:44, 65). Technically and legally, the door is open and the invitation is extended to all that they may enter. But spiritually and actually, none can move towards or through that door unless he has divine enablement. All are like the paralysed man at the pool in Bethesda who said, 'I have no man... to put me into the pool.' Man has a will, but in relationship to the things of God it is paralysed.

It is not without significance that in this twentieth century since our Lord was here on earth the human race has become characterized by a mania over 'rights'. In the political, educational, financial, domestic and legal spheres, a considerable amount of time and energy is wasted over battles as to whose 'rights' may have been transgressed in any given incident, or in any legislative action that may be proposed. While there is a legitimate place for this in many areas, it is altogether out of its reasonable position when these so-called 'rights' interfere with God's ordained institutions and his order of procedure in each. The prodigal son well illustrates this rebellious attitude. He said, 'Father give me...' It was more of a demand than a request. Though spoken over 2,000 years ago, this is as up-to-date as today's newspaper.

The prodigal's attitude is soon revealed by his actions. His imperious demand was quickly followed by his departure from home and family. His feelings about the restraints of his father's house were soon made plain when in 'the far country' he carried out in action what he could only dream about while under his father's roof. Removal of restraint, or a removal from it, will expose what has long been hidden in the heart.

This is a vivid picture of the sinner's inner life. He chafes at restrictions and seeks to escape what he regards as their tyranny over his natural freedom. Man by nature is lawless. If he conforms to certain rules and regulations to gain some greater end, he is constantly irritated by the necessity of doing so. Were he free (as he supposes) he would arrive at true liberty. But consider the prodigal. Release from his parent's jurisdiction did not result in the liberty he fantasized about.

When he achieved his coveted desire he became more en-
slaved to others than he had imagined himself to be in his
father's house. Far better to have remained under the government of one who loved him than to have become the servant
of another who despised him.

His life-style became hedonistic and this resulted in an enslavement to his own lusts. 'He wasted his substance with
riotous living.' Man, apart from divine grace, and left to
himself, will normally give free rein to his worst propensities.
He soon learns how to spend his resources, but he knows little
about how to accumulate them. The prodigal 'lived up' his
capital rather quickly.

The severity of his conviction

Remembering that all three accounts teach the same thing, and
that the whole parable is entirely consistent with the doctrines
of grace clearly expounded in many other Scriptures, we may
observe how Christ emphatically taught that 'Salvation is of
the Lord.' The prodigal's rescue from a dreaded end is quite
consistent with what our Lord set out under the two previous
narratives.

The prodigal was a son before he left for the 'far country'.
He was a son all the while he was in that alien culture, and he
was a son when he was ushered back into the safety and
sanctity of the father's house upon his return. From the
moment, years before, that his father had registered him in the
family records until the time that he escorted him back within
the ancestral halls, he never ceased to be a 'son' in the mind of
his father, and it is most certain that those records were never
changed. Though while separated from the father's house he
was considered as 'lost', and even 'dead', there was still a bond
that could not be broken because it was established in the heart
of the father. Even so, what God has determined in the
counsels of eternity cannot be altered. Whom he has

predestinated he also calls, justifies and glorifies (Rom. 8:29-30). When the elder son retorted to his father, 'this thy son...' in referring to his errant brother, he revealed that the father had continued to consider him as such all the while he was gone from home. No doubt the petulant rejoinder was based upon the father's habitual way of referring to him.

Just as the sheep always belonged to the shepherd, though for a time it was lost, and exactly as the coin was properly the woman's personal possession, though for a time it could not be found, so the prodigal son was continuously the son of his father, in spite of the fact that he was under his temporary displeasure. Indeed, had the father's country been at war with the 'far country', the prodigal could well have been put to death by an invading army from his homeland. His position had put him at enmity with the government under which his father functioned at home. But it was grace that brought him back into his father's house.

On the biblical basis that we become 'sons of God' in the new birth and cannot be accounted as such before that (Eph. 2; Rom. 5), the logical question is raised: 'How does this fit the pattern?' Or to put it another way, 'Is this not incipient liberalism, that people may be considered "sons of God" before they have been regenerated by the Holy Spirit?'Someone might also ask, 'Is this teaching not essentially the Reformed view of the "covenant child" who may wander away but will always come back?'

These are logical questions and deserve consideration. In the first place, since it is only one parable, and not three, it becomes evident that each section must teach the same thing. The Lord did not teach in self-contradictory figures of speech. The prodigal must be what both the sheep and the coin were. In the second place, it is quite different from liberalism which teaches that all mankind are children of God on the basis of their birth into the human race. The sonship taught in the parable is not that of mere biological descent, but that of sovereign election arranged by God. In the third place, this differs radically from the Reformed view of the 'covenant child' in that this concept assumes the existence of such a thing as a 'covenant family' (which is unknown to the New Testament), and that infant 'baptism' somehow brings the child into a relationship with the kingdom of Christ.

The sonship of the prodigal was based upon an action completely outside himself. It speaks of our spiritual relationship to God which is brought about entirely apart from any action on our part or from any procedure arranged for us by proxy. This rests entirely upon the decree of sovereign election. In the eternal records of God, those who come to be recognized publicly as his children here on earth were prophetically his children long before they were born into the human family. The desertion of the father's house in the parable speaks of our wilful flight from the government of God immediately we began to operate as individuals. Our depravity manifests itself in our very first behaviour.

The inspired record tells us that without delay infants manifest their rebellious nature (Ps. 58:3). All humans go astray 'from the womb', and all parents who are honest with themselves will admit to the truth of this. Those who have been born in our households, though they may be the elect of God, manifest the same wilful and rebellious nature as do the others of the neighbourhood who are non-elect. Though they are scheduled in God's plan for regeneration and complete revolution of life, they will manifest the common depravity before that miraculous event takes place. The elect child will travel into 'the far country' as soon as he can escape the government of the father's house. Or (if he can manage it) he may rebelliously reject the family discipline while he is still there. Blessed are those homes where the order and godly examples are such that this journey is not too far away from proper influence. Especially blessed are those households where the excursion into the alien land is terminated before the children are of an age to demand their legal freedom and operate in total independence of parental guidance. Happily, most homes which are properly ordered and disciplined will experience this happy spiritual 'return' before the children ever leave the shelter of their immediate family.

But the return does not take place until the prodigal is driven to an extremity of some kind. There are two salient features to the story our Lord told, each of which illustrates one of the aspects of spiritual conviction of sin. Here we see the exercise of soul through which an elect person will travel before it can be said that he 'came to himself'.

The Lord said that at the time when the prodigal's resources had become exhausted, 'A mighty famine arose in the land.' This speaks of *God's sovereign control of all circumstances which surround the elect* (Rom. 8:28-30). In order to bring the errant son to the realization of his danger, providence arranged that the depletion of his capital would coincide with the period of great dearth which touched all in the land.

The prodigal knew well how to spend money, but he was ignorant of how to earn it. This implies that he had learned very little in his ancestral home from his father's evident success and prosperity. No doubt his interests did not lie in the direction of the accumulation of wealth, but in the selfish enjoyment of hastily squandering it. When this is applied to the lesson it is intended to teach, it suggests that children in our homes have an unusual opportunity to learn about the 'true riches' of the Scriptures and the important wealth of spiritual principles. Natural human depravity is manifested in their dullness about these things until they are regenerated. How often they neglect their advantages to learn how to cope with life until they have wandered far from home! So it was with the prodigal.

The famine was no accident. In Scripture calamitous dearth is usually presented as the consequence of spiritual declension or rebellion. Christ is showing that the Father will regulate all the circumstances which may surround the elect to bring them to the place of realization. The 'predestination' of which Paul speaks (Rom. 8:29; Eph. 1:5,11) focuses upon the circumstances which encompass the earthly sojourn of the elect to bring them into the realization of their plight and their need of rescue. Again, this is how it was with the prodigal. He was in ignorance of his danger until he began to feel the pinch of the circumstances.

The second thing of interest to our exposition is the fact that *the prodigal attempted to solve his problems by his own efforts*. After he had felt the effects of the divinely arranged famine, he made attempts to remedy the situation by joining himself to a citizen of the 'far country' in order to work for a living. He was willing to do anything but go back home.

When a man begins to feel the pinch of divinely arranged circumstances which have been predestined to 'hedge up his way with thorns', this is usually his immediate reaction. He devises schemes involving strenuous effort or distasteful duty as an attempt to compensate for the lack he experiences. Pilgrimages, public humiliation, painful exercises of soul and various forms of legalistic self-abasement have been employed by various religious groups in an attempt to assuage the pangs of conscience and line the coffers of the professionals.

The 'citizen of the far country' to whom he joined himself may well represent the religious charlatans of any age who profit by the psychological problems of the person under a deep realization of his spiritual need, who in desperation seeks help in the immediately proffered aid rather than going through the agonizing process of self-examination in the light of what has actually happened to him. The journey to his father's house seems too long. The feeding of swine, as humiliating as it must have been, appeared far preferable to the rough road back home. As yet he could have no concept of the fact that the father would give him such a wonderful welcome.

The prodigal son was found and restored

The recovery of the lost son is, equally with the other stories, a picture of experienced salvation. This may be seen in two aspects: first his restoration to correct thinking, and second his restoration to proper living. The first part of the narrative depicts the mental processes through which the mind under spiritual conviction must go; the second shows the undeserved and unexpected reception from his Father against whom he has transgressed. This section will be devoted to the first consideration.

In the case of the sheep, the finding was all on the part of the shepherd. In the case of the coin it was all on the part of the woman as guided by the light she held. But in the instance of the prodigal there is no search mounted and no external invasion by presence or by voice. How does this illustrate the doctrines of grace?

In our Lord's narrative the focus is directed to two things: the external circumstances and the internal conflict. The first suggests to us the situations into which someone may be born or into which he seems later to thrust himself. The prodigal set about to enjoy life to the fullest according to his distorted view of what it really was. In wasting his substance with riotous living he evidenced the concepts of life ordinarily held in the minds of unregenerate people.

The dedication to the pursuit of pleasure is motivated by

the notion that this in itself can bring happiness. However, the prodigal did not find it so. He began to be in want. He was deserted by his erstwhile friends. Just so, the individual who devotes his life to a satisfaction of the senses (intellectually, emotionally, or physically) will sooner or later come to the end of that folly. And in the event that he should be one of God's elect, some providential circumstances beyond his control will be brought into his experience, often painfully. At this point his 'friends' will be of no comfort to him.

However, unaware that the famine experienced by every-one, which seemed to have come out of nowhere, had a direct bearing upon him in his present condition, he still attempted to rationalize. The famine pinched. Since he had dedicated him-self to the pursuit of pleasure, providential circumstances spoke to him in the only language which he was able to under-stand. God began with him where he was. Having been living only for the satisfaction of the senses, he now felt the move-ment of God into his life in this area. He suffered hunger. His mind began to awaken to his desperate condition.

This portion of the parable illustrates the mental and emotional struggles through which an elect person may go when God begins to move into his sphere of experience. Since the prodigal lived entirely for himself, with a dedication to the pursuit of pleasure, he first felt the invasion of providence in that area of his sensibilities. He had been living with physical satisfaction uppermost in mind. That came to an abrupt end with the rise of the famine in the land. While one may not see such hardship as a direct intervention of God, taken in the context and larger view of his control (in predestination) of all circumstances towards the realization in our experience of our salvation (election), this conforms to the biblical revelation of how the Father may begin to reach the people whom he has chosen (Rom. 8:20-31).

This explains why no one is sent for the son. Our Lord wants us to understand that while it is true that the Son does seek, as a Shepherd, and that while the Spirit does search, as

a light, yet the overriding control is located in the purpose of
the Father, who orders and arranges everything because he
'worketh all things after the counsel of his own will' (Eph.
1:11). Here we see that even the natural or physical circumstances which surround us are all made to work towards our
realization of salvation by grace (Rom. 8:28).

This parable must be understood in the light of its setting.
The background is Hebrew. No pious Jew ever considered a
famine as an accident. He had been thoroughly instructed,
both from a multitude of passages in the law and the prophets,
and from the careful education in rabbinical thought patterns,
that such things were indeed 'acts of God'. Those who heard
that parable, from their knowledge of the Old Testament,
would immediately attribute the words, 'There arose a mighty
famine in that land...' to refer to exactly that kind of divine
judgement for sin (Deut. 28-30; 2 Kings 8:1; Ps. 105:16; Isa.
14:30; Ezek. 5:16, etc.). The Jewish tradition, based upon such
inspired passages, was reflected in the apocryphal writings
(and the teachings of the rabbis as well). Christ's hearers
would have understood that.

The prodigal's reaction to the famine was not immediately what it should have been. Rather than examining his own
heart, he resorted to his active mind, and he devised a scheme
of self-salvation which he believed would ease his immediate
suffering and perhaps ultimately deliver him from the threat he
voiced, 'I perish...' He joined himself to one of the local
citizens of the 'far country' who proffered a miserable survival
on the condition that he would work as a swineherd. Evidently
the 'citizen' did not provide properly for his physical needs
and the prodigal was hungry to the point of imagined star-
vation, and no one had any concern for his pitiful condition.
'No man gave unto him.'

The 'far country' of this world has no lack of these
'citizens' who have made a business of providing such
arrangements for the enslavement of people who have come to
feel their need of help. Ranging all the way from the naturalistic

schools of humanistic psychology to the occult sects of demonic activity, they have two common denominators. They require that the person 'work' for his own deliverance from the 'famine', and they do not deliver what they promise.

The 'citizen' of our Lord's parable 'sent him into his fields to feed swine' (v. 15). As a Jewish youth he had been taught to have nothing to do with these animals, but now in his desperation he was willing to throw away his childhood standards. He actually enlisted as a member of this person's work-force.

The prodigal joined himself to an individual who operated a business which proved to be degrading to the young man's true heritage. He had not been brought into the world for this purpose. There was an infinitely higher end in view. On the natural plane, he might have had his proper heritage at home and never have been reduced to the penury and shame of this abasement. This speaks of the many and varied forms of human experience with the numerous religions of this world. It also stands as a warning against departure from the standards of truth in Scripture. Such desertion of truth is fraught with infinite dangers.

The prodigal first became aware of the work of God in his physical experience, brought on by the providential famine. Many of the elect have had to suffer in a physical way before coming to Christ. The testimonies of numerous people are that they were apprehended by the Lord in a serious illness, a tragic bereavement, a disastrous loss, or some combination of these things. Tragic though it may be, quite often it is true to experience. Man does not learn until he feels pain.

The turning point of the parable comes after the acute misery was suffered. Following his descent to the point where he 'would fain have filled his belly with the husks that the swine did eat', he had a remarkable experience. Some people do not begin to think until they realize that they have descended to the level of animals. It is not stated that he actually ate the food of swine, but that he was hungry enough seriously to contemplate it. Sometimes humans startle themselves with what they seriously consider. In some instances it becomes a means of their awakening.

However, the actual point of his 'about face' does not occur until 'he came to himself'. It is at that point, and not before, that some thoughts of 'the father's house' first entered his thought processes. But the first conscious perception following this great metamorphosis was of the vast gulf that separated him from his father's house. 'How many hired servants of my father's have bread enough and to spare, and I perish with hunger!' (v.17). He had not even thought of his ancestral home during his downward plunge. Now for the first time since leaving its precincts his mind turned towards the place of peace, security and prosperity.

From this point onwards the prodigal underwent a radical change. His thought processes were revolutionary. Contrasting the two attitudes represented in his downward and upward courses, and locating the change precisely at the time 'when he came to himself', we see that in the application of the allegory this change evidently represents regeneration. Before that moment he had no thought of the father's house. Now his mind was filled with it.

Prior to this time he had used the word 'father' only once (v.12), and that was only in a strictly legal sense devoid of any love or filial loyalty. It was a mere formality which was demanded by the custom of the times. He used the term 'father' only to get what his impetuous nature desired.

But now the word 'father' appears repeatedly in his mind. His first spiritually conscious thought included it (v. 17). His determination to go back was formed into a sentence: 'I will arise and go to my father...' (v. 18). His carefully considered and penitent speech began with the words: 'Father, I have sinned...' (v. 18). He had not thought in such terms since leaving home, and probably had never seriously considered his status before that, but now his mind was filled with the realization that he was a son of a father.

Paul puts this into Christian doctrine in his epistles. Typical of this are two significant passages on fatherhood and sonship which have come into full realization with the institution of the New Covenant. The apostle reminds his readers that it is by the Spirit of God that we have this sense of sonship. This points to our regeneration (Rom. 8:14-17; Gal. 4:4-7).

Assuming that the words, 'He came to himself', represent the point in the parable where regeneration is indicated, it then conforms to these passages in the epistles where we are taught that the consciousness of our sonship and the realization of God's fatherhood come with regeneration. Before that moment we were *not* sons, nor was he our Father, except in prospect. But with the miracle comes the blessing of this twofold consciousness. While multitudes of ritualistic 'worshippers' have often used the word 'father' in a mere ceremonial sense with no actual appreciation of its specific meaning, when the elect are regenerated they are quite mysteriously and miraculously taught this truth. The sense of fatherhood and the realization of sonship are the immediate products of regenerating grace. This consciousness is not conveyed by education or ceremony. It is unknown to the world, as it was unknown by experience to national Israel before the institution of the New Covenant (Jer. 31:33-34; Heb. 7-13; 10:15-23). In the two passages from Paul's epistles already mentioned, this sense of sonship and divine fatherhood is attributed to the work of the Holy Spirit. It was this new attitude in the heart and mind of the prodigal which redirected him to arise and come to his father (v. 20). From an observer's point of view it would have seemed that the young man had no outside assistance in arriving at this conclusion. Quite unlike the sheep whose shepherd appeared on the scene, and obviously in contrast to the coin whose rescue was accomplished by the means of light in the hands of the woman, the prodigal seemed to be quite alone in the whole procedure. You could not have observed any influence operating upon him in any sense.

This very well illustrates the invincible power of God that

works effectually to bring the elect to him. Paul's words put it in language which refers to 'the exceeding greatness of his power to us-ward who believe, according to the working of his mighty power...' (Eph. 1:19). The elect will infallibly come to Christ. The prodigal will 'arise and go'. Since 'all things work together for good' for the ones who are 'called according to his purpose', this cannot fail. He who is registered as a son in the records of heaven (by sovereign election) will come to the realization of his sonship in experience. This starts with his regeneration, in which he is divinely taught to say, 'Abba, Father'. It is pictured in the parable as the point where the prodigal 'came to himself'.

It is now important to concentrate upon the difference between the son's fears of rejection and the attitude of the father. The prodigal, in the realization of his past, rehearsed a speech of penitence. He was quite willing to take the lowest place in the father's house, just so that he could get inside. He went over the words that he would say: 'Father, I have sinned ... and am no more worthy to be called thy son: make me as one of thy hired servants' (v.19). This he said while still in the 'far country' and no doubt he rehearsed it again on the way home. The important point is that he did arise and return to the father.

The prodigal's attitude was one of true penitence, and he returned to plead for mercy. He would seek for no higher place than that of a slave in the father's domains, if indeed, he could be received at all. He must have been aware that he had no legal right to any place whatever. All the legitimate 'rights' had already been collected and forfeited at his departure some time before. He had no prerogative. His legal status had been surrendered earlier. Just like Esau, he had sold his birthright. He could have no expectation that he would fare any better than that unhappy elder brother of the patriarch. But he must go home. He could not bear to do otherwise. An inexorable force within was driving him.

True repentance causes a soul to seek for mercy. Such a soul comes to God in the knowledge that the holy Judge of the universe has every right to condemn him and cast him away. But come he must. His approach should be with some fear and trembling in view of the great spiritual facts involved.

In our days of careless religious exercises there is almost no sense of this involved in the ministry ordinarily called 'evangelistic'. It would be far better for the cause of truth and the fulfilment of the Great Commission if souls were taught to approach the throne of God with fear and trembling. During previous times of genuine revival the testimonies were more often of this nature. I can remember reading of the many who, under the preaching during the Great Awakening, approached God with the thought that if sending them to hell would glorify God, then they were willing that this should be done to them. The prodigal had as yet no knowledge of the response he would receive from his father. He would learn that in time. But no doubt the road homeward was undertaken with some fear and dread.

The reception of the prodigal deserves careful attention. The Father's heart is now revealed. How does God look upon sinners who are divinely directed to come to him? Christ expounds this in the parable. Several aspects merit study.

1.   The father waits for the return of the prodigal

The Lord pointed out that long before the son arrived in the vicinity of the house he was espied on the roadway. 'But when he was yet a great way off *his* [not merely 'the'] father saw him...' (v.20). Observe that it was not a servant who came in from the field with this news, which would be the ordinary experience, but the father himself who first caught sight of the boy.

This indicates that the sorrowing parent had probably mounted a regular watch upon the housetop to be able to see his returning son when he was still only a small object upon the horizon. The heavenly Father loves the ones who are 'the called according to his purpose', but who have strayed far off the path of righteousness and possibly into great sin. In telling out the heart of the Father, our Lord presents the story with full emotional overtones. God is not merely a sovereign controller of all circumstances concerned in our election. He is intensely involved in a personal, emotional way. 'Herein is love, not that we loved God, but that he loved us, and sent his Son to be the propitiation for our sins' (1 John 4:10). God's love for us is beyond our ability to understand.

2. The Father personally welcomes the son into the fold

It would have been sufficient if the father in the parable had waited for the prodigal to arrive at the gate and have his presence announced within, and then had made him wait outside until his application for employment was processed. The boy could have expected no more than that in his highest hopes. But his change of attitude was so complete that he would have been happy even with such a decision.

But our Lord does not present the father in such a detached position. On the contrary, when the head of the household finally espied his lost son on the horizon, he *ran* (not 'walked') from his place of long surveillance, through the house, across the courtyard, out of the gate and down the road. Dignity was temporarily laid aside, probably to the shock of the servants who had never seen him do anything like this before.

Can we who are proud of our firm position in the doctrines of grace grasp this concept? Can Calvinists conceive of the mental images brought up by the thought of God's running to greet a repentant sinner? Are we sometimes so impressed with the medieval scholasticism which tends to attach to some of our theological acumen that we do not understand what our Lord was saying here? Have we absorbed so much of the stereotyped formalism which has traditionally attached to the words 'Puritan' and/or 'Reformed' that we recoil at this concept? But our Lord did not hesitate to tell this story to reveal the heart of the Father and to spend much more time on it than on the other two accounts. Could it be that in our determination to correct the Arminian distortions of God we have unconsciously created some of our own?

3.   The Father identifies himself with the errant son

It would have been gracious if the father in the story had simply called to the youth from his vantage-point on top of the house and had requested that he come inside, take a bath and appear before him when he was properly cleansed and attired. Grace would have provided a room, and even servants, to help him in this preparation. That would have been considerably above what the prodigal had a right to expect.

But in contrast to David and his aloofness from Absalom (2 Sam. 14), the father in Christ's parable ran out to meet the boy who had returned with the marks of his recent occupation upon him. Disregarding for the moment the evidences of his degrading servitude, the father flung his arms about the boy and kissed him. The *heart* of the Father is being expounded here. The repentance in the soul of the prodigal far outweighs his appearance. The father in the parable made no remonstrance for the son's abysmally bad behaviour. No doubt this had been mentioned by the elder son in the father's presence, as is indicated by his petulant remark later (v. 30). Since it had been in the mind of the elder son during his brother's absence, it is inconceivable that he had not 'cast it up' to his father from time to time. But the loving reception included none of this.

4.   The Father graciously provides for the prodigal's needs

Grace is seen in every word and line of this account. Whereas the son had begun his carefully rehearsed speech which had been composed in the 'far country', the father did not allow him to continue. The son's penitent words were interrupted at a significant point. He had planned to ask for the position of a hired servant (v.19). But before he could utter these words, the father halted his recital with the gracious words: 'Bring forth the best robe, and put it on him; and put a ring on his hand, and shoes on his feet...' (v. 22).

The rejoicing father ushered his returned son back into the household with the joyous words: 'And bring hither the fatted calf, and kill it; and let us eat, and be merry: for this my son was dead, and is alive again; he was lost, and is found' (v. 23). This accords with the notes of joy sounded in each of the separate stories (vv. 6-7, 9-10). It is evident that our Lord intended to teach here that God's heart rejoices in the salvation of the lost. It is one of the most outstanding facts of the parable.

God's grace is obvious in all parts of the parable. It would have been most gracious of the father to have given the returned prodigal a servant's place and thus rescue him from the just rewards of his previous escapade in the 'far country'. But to have elevated him to his former estate, to have reinstated him with such a celebration, and not merely to have joined in the festivities, but to have initiated them himself, is 'grace abounding to the chief of sinners'. Calvinists are frequently accused of having a concept of God which is all judgement and austerity. They are maligned as holding to mental images of God which are cold, heartless and unsmiling. But this perception is not based upon the observation of those who sincerely believe the doctrines of grace and act accordingly. While there are, and have been, Calvinists who can well be characterized by this distorted caricature, this is not true of the ones who understand our Lord's teaching about grace.

5.   The father rejoices with the son

Immediately upon his return the prodigal was properly cleansed from the former life and appropriately attired. He entered into a time of celebration along with the father and the others of the household (with one exception).

While the returned son was welcomed home without any condemnatory remonstrance, he was not restored without being cleansed and properly attired in new garments. Truly repentant sinners are to be welcomed into Christian fellowship, but it must be evident that they are genuinely contrite of heart; nor are the garments of 'the far country', much less its manners and odours, acceptable within the sacred precincts.

Sometimes churches err on the side of excluding some who should be received, perhaps more on grounds of culture than on evidence of life (Rom. 14:1-6). On the other hand, some churches blunder in lowering the biblical standards to the point where the values of the world are too readily absorbed. The people who enjoy the fellowship of 'the father's house' will enjoy the celebrations involved within this holy company, but their festivities will neither look nor sound the same as the ones so recently enjoyed by the prodigal in the 'far country'. Unhappily, too many churches of our time have attempted to look and sound so much like the world that one has difficulty in discerning any difference. When the music of a Christian radio station sounds almost exactly like that which comes from the popular 'rock stations' one has reason to fear that this blunder has been made.

The prodigal son was maligned

Only in the third story does our Lord refer to the Pharisaic reaction against God's grace. With both the rescued sheep and the restored coin there was only rejoicing. But with the recovered son a sour note was sounded. The elder son refused to join in with the others of the household as they joyfully celebrated the return of the younger son.

However, it was not only a festival of joy over his recovery; it was also a glad occasion of rejoicing in the grace of the father who gladly forgave his errant son. If we can picture the account, as our Lord certainly intended that we should, we can hear various testimonies mingle with the songs that sounded throughout the great house that evening. The most important of these were thoughts that celebrated the father's grace. As it was with the shepherd, so it was with the father. The more significant focus is upon the one who sought and found and the one who forgave and restored.

From our human standpoint we usually place emphasis upon the object rescued, but from the divine perspective the emphasis should rather be on the one who does the rescuing. The shepherd found and rescued the sheep, the light located the coin and the father forgave the son. It would seem that the most mature testimonies of praise that happy evening in the great hall were directed to the person who made it all possible and who demonstrated his love in his actions.

But there was an unhappy person who belonged to that household who could not enter into the joy of the occasion. The elder son, upon hearing of the father's mercy and forgiveness and of the celebration, petulantly refused to have anything to do with the festivities. We remember that the Pharisees were present when our Lord taught this lesson (v. 2).

Christ now directs the parable to them. The prodigal son represented the 'publicans and sinners' who were present (v. 1), many of whom had come to trust in the Saviour. The 'elder son' represented the Pharisees, most of whom had been nursing a grudge against him. Just as the 'elder son' had never entered into the heart interest of the father, so had the Pharisees completely missed the knowledge of God's love in redemption. Yet there is an appeal made to them.

With regard to the elder son a number of points should be made.

1.   *He had been in covenant relationship with the father.* This comes to light in the appeal which was made to him. He is reminded that 'All that I have is thine' (v. 31). National Israel, as represented by the scribes and Pharisees, had enjoyed this covenant bond ever since the days of Abraham. This had been the subject of much Old Testament writing, both in history and in prophecy (e.g. Exod. 19-20; Deut. 28-30; 2 Sam. 7:1-17; Dan. 9:24-27).

However, far from humbly acknowledging that this was God's gracious provision for them, they proudly imagined that in some way it had been a reward for their self-righteousness. God's grace in redemption had been almost completely missed, so that when the Saviour appeared their natural hatred of grace was plainly expressed in their animosity towards him.

2.   *A direct and personal appeal was made to him by the father.* Upon hearing of his first son's negative reaction to the news of grace extended to the prodigal, the father left the

celebrations and went out to speak with his first-born. 'Therefore came his father out, and intreated him' (v. 28).

God spoke to Israel through his Son during the days of Christ's earthly ministry. The nation's answer was rejection and crucifixion. But even so, after the New Covenant had been instituted in Jesus' blood and executed by the advent of the Holy Spirit, the message went first to Israel. The early days of the church in Jerusalem were occupied with witnessing to this nation. From Acts 2 until the seventh chapter all is Jewish. The apostle Paul continually sought out his brethren according to the flesh, and in one verse tells the story of the earliest days of the gospel ministry — 'to the Jew first' (Rom. 1:16). The father's entreaty carried outdoors to the elder son is a prophecy in typology for this very thing.

3. *The elder son's attitude was one of servitude.* In his ill-tempered response he pointed to his years of service as deserving what his brother was now receiving, but declared his sense of injustice in that what he thought he had earned he had never really enjoyed. But his younger sibling, the 'black sheep' of the family, was now given this exalted position which should have been his by right. His anger at both the father and the brother is clearly seen.

This is precisely what Israel did with God's grace. Not only were they angry with the 'publicans and sinners' whom Christ received during his ministry, but they were angry with God for permitting it to happen. This anger came out clearly in the crucifixion of Christ, and then it turned to the early church which preached grace. Paul's most vicious enemies were those of the Pharasiac party, and there are many evidences of this in the book of Acts as well as the epistles.

The preaching and teaching of the gospel of pure grace, i.e. the announcement of the evangel in the context of the doctrines of grace, meet with the same reception today. Whereas two millennia ago the enemies of grace were clearly identified as a religious party within Israel (the Pharisees), in these days there is no such clear distinction. The works-oriented self-righteousness spirit has invaded many different forms of credal statements and religious establishments. They have one common mark. They exalt the human capability to the detriment of the grace of God. This animosity towards grace may be formally expressed, as it is in some of the more liturgical denominations of Christendom which require some sacramental ceremony as necessary to salvation. It may be represented in those religious systems which require some continuous obedience to a codification of law (be it the decalogue or some humanly devised scheme of legislation) to merit salvation. But the picture of the elder brother in this parable illustrates the works-oriented attitude towards salvation. The blessings of God's grace are allowed to come only when man has done something to merit that reward.

Man is naturally prone to this attitude. Adam, upon becoming aware of his condition of being out of fellowship with God, began to sew fig leaves together in order to make himself presentable again. But this was by his own work and could not suffice. His covering was, in grace, provided by God himself, when he made coats of skins for the objects of his love and then clothed them with what he had provided (Gen. 3:21).

Conclusion

The parable of the lost things is Christ's own revelation of the heart of the triune God regarding his redemption of lost man. It states or implies the manner in which that story, which is the gospel of grace, should be propagated throughout the world. It should be at the heart of our programmes of evangelism and missionary endeavour. All our efforts in evangelistic work should conform to the principles clearly established in this parable. Departures from these concepts spell eventual ruin to the execution of the Great Commission, both at home and abroad.

References

Chapter 2

1. Benjamin Keach, *Exposition of the Parables* (Kregel, 1974; reprint ed., 1856), p. 349.

Chapter 3

1. R. C. Trench, *Notes on the Parables of our Lord*, Appleton, 1857, p. 312.

2. An antidote to this misunderstanding is a careful study of Christ's words about the Spirit in John 14-16. He repeatedly refers to the Holy Spirit with the pronoun 'he'.

3. A. B. Bruce, 'The Synoptic Gospels', *The Expositor's Greek Testament*, Eerdmans, p. 579.

4. W. S. Hottel, 'Christ's Concern for the Lost,' *Bible Expositor and Illuminator*, 1940, Lesson 4, p.50.